# Old Loch Goil

Mark Morpurgo & Caroline Wilson

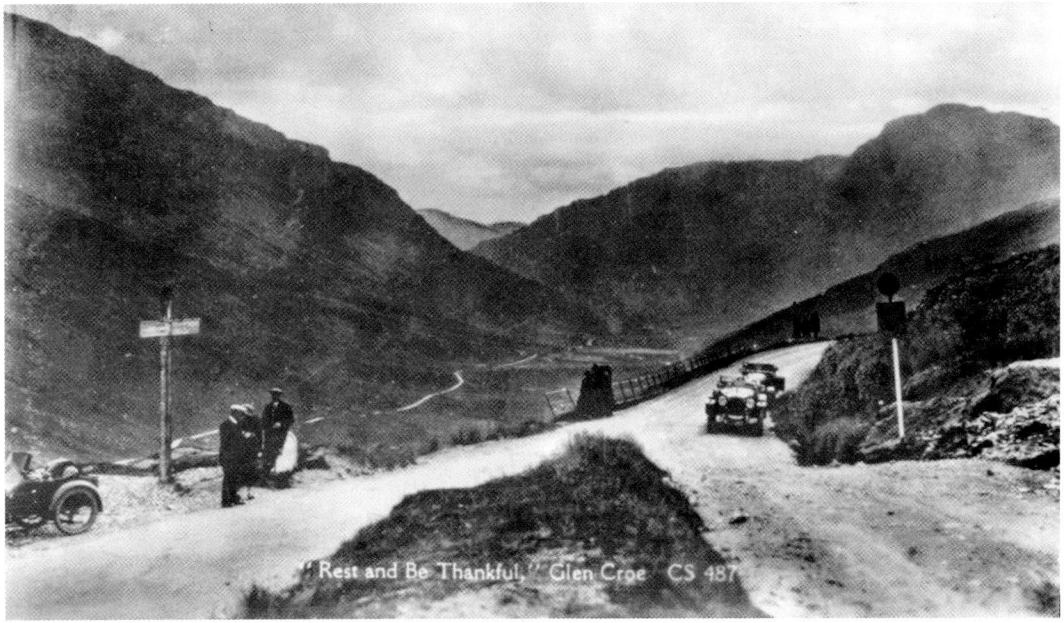


The poet John Keats was probably not the first traveller, or the last, to think that there was an inn, or refreshments, at the top of the Rest and Be Thankful and on 17 July 1818 wrote – 'We were up at four this morning and have walked to breakfast fifteen miles through two tremendous glens; at the head of the first there is a place called Rest and Be Thankful, which we took for an inn; it was nothing but a stone and we were cheated into five more miles to breakfast'.

The stone he refers to was erected in 1748 by a mason with General Wade's company of engineers and can still be seen next to the modern car park. After the strenuous activity of building the road up Glen Croe it is not surprising that he carved a message inviting travellers to Rest and Be Thankful. Later information on the stone states that the road was repaired in 1768 by the 93rd Regiment and that in 1814 it was transferred to the responsibility of the Commissioners for Highland Roads and Bridges.

In 1803 Dorothy Wordsworth, together with her brother William, made a similar trip to Keats, but by carriage and pony. She records seeing the farm buildings in the glen, the only habitation they saw on their journey. This view, dating from the 1920s, shows cars having made the ascent. The Baedeker guide of the time advised drivers to go up the hill in reverse!

First Published in the United Kingdom, 2006
Stenlake Publishing Limited
54–58 Mill Square
Catrine
KA5 6RD
www.stenlake.co.uk

ISBN 1 84033 373 1

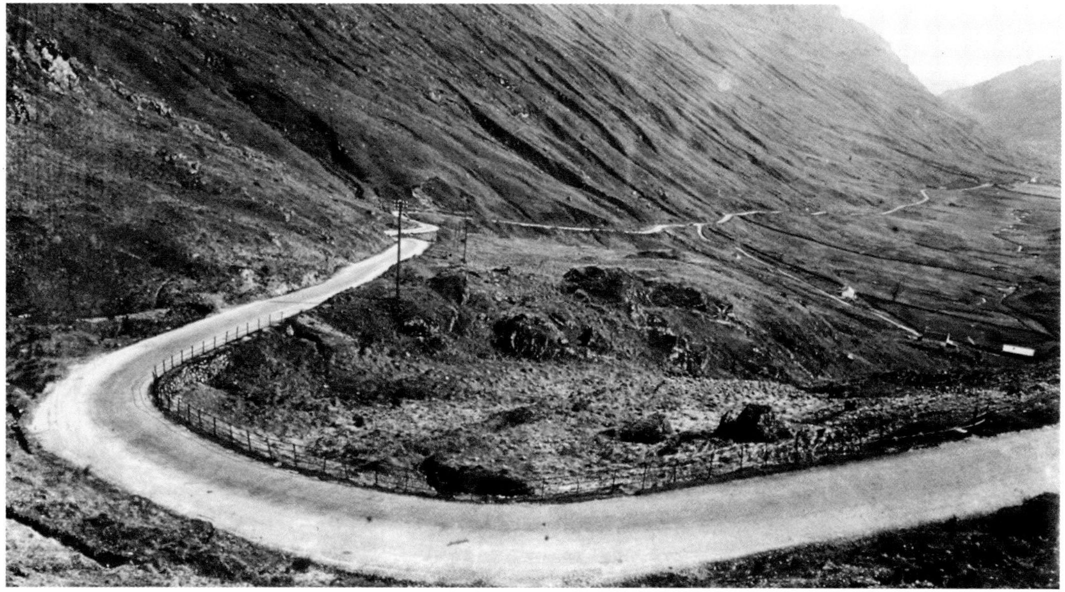

The Union of the Parliaments was looked on by Scotland as an unpleasant necessity whereby she had 'surrendered much and received little in return'. Measures for the pacification and disarmament of the country after the 1715 rising had been of limited success. In 1724 General George Wade, who was the real pioneer of Highland road building, came to Scotland and over the following four years built close on 250 miles of roads in the Highlands – an extraordinary engineering feat using mainly unskilled labour and primitive tools. Militarily it was less successful. He had gone north charged with the task of disarming the rebellion and subduing the Highlands yet, in 1745, five years after he left, the clans rose again with weapons he had failed to confiscate and Bonnie Prince Charlie was using the very road system that Wade had built.

Although the military roads are usually referred to as 'Wade' roads, the section below the Rest and Be Thankful was built by military labour under the direction of Edward Caulfield, Inspector of Roads. The Wade road can be seen below the Rest and Be Thankful in this 1920s photo.

## INTRODUCTION

For several hundred years Lochgoilhead and Carrick Castle on Loch Goil were part of the estate of the Campbells of Ardkinglas (which at one point also covered Strachur, Glendaruel, Kilmun, Dunoon and Toward) and thus were connected with Cairndow, near the head of Loch Fyne. The founder of the house of Ardkinglas was one Colin Campbell, who in 1396 was granted the lands by his father (also Colin Campbell) 'on condition that he should keep at his own expences two War-Galleys, one of eight oars, the other of six to serve the Lord of Lochow and the King of the Scots in times of tumult and war'. For at least a century before that, however, the area was possessed by the parent house Campbell of Loch Awe/Campbell of Argyll.

It was the fourth Laird of Ardkinglas, Iain Campbell, who endowed the chantry altar in Lochgoilhead Church in 1512. Just over a year later he was buried there, one of the casualties of Flodden. An elaborate Renaissance monument in the church commemorates the ninth Laird, James Campbell, and the lairds continued to be buried in the church until the middle of the nineteenth century. In 1752, however, the direct male line had failed on the death of James Campbell, the eleventh Laird. The succession passed through his daughter Helen to the Livingstone family and then to the Callendars (although some of them took on the Campbell name). The fifteenth Laird spent most of his time abroad on account of his debts, and by the time of his death in 1851 Ardkinglas itself was heavily burdened. The seventeenth and final Laird, George Frederick William Callendar, was forced to dispose of the property in parts. In 1905 Sir Andrew Noble purchased what was left of the main estate and Mr Cameron Corbett acquired the smaller Ardgoil portion, which he then gifted to Glasgow Corporation.

The old name of the parish of Lochgoilhead was *Kil nam brathairan* (the church is known as 'the church of the three brethren'), but from the late 1600s the settlement was known as Lochgoil-head or Kinlochgoil. Its importance in the eighteenth century was due to its being on the main route from northern Argyll to Glasgow and the south. At that time travel was by horseback or by foot and by boat. Lochgoilhead would have been a principal resting place en route. Apart from the running of sheep, a major source of income, according to the *Statistical Account of Scotland* (written by the Rev. Dugal McDougal in 1791), was the fishing industry. The whiting, haddock, mackerel and cod caught in Loch Goil and Loch Long could easily be transported to Greenock, Port Glasgow, Paisley and Glasgow. In the 1790s up to 500 men and 120 boats were involved. Fishing also took place on Loch Fyne, whose herring was carried in creels on horseback via Hell's Glen to Lochgoilhead for shipping to the towns.

With the arrival of steamers in the early nineteenth century, Lochgoilhead remained a major transport hub, as it enjoyed a regular service. However, the demand for food for the workers in the expanding industrial towns meant that a more direct way of transporting Argyll's fish was required and so the 'herring roads' were built. One of the earliest was the Hell's Glen road from Loch Fyne to Lochgoilhead. Improved road transportation meant that the Loch Goil and Loch Long Steamboat Company was able in 1829 to set up a ferry service from St. Catherine's across Loch Fyne, permitting tourists to journey from Glasgow or Greenock to Inveraray. The advent of the railways also boosted the tourist trade. A tour for the more enterprising was to arrive at Lochgoilhead, walk over the Rest and Be Thankful and Ben Arthur and return by the Arrochar steamer. Another of the most popular was known as the Three Lochs Tour, which cruised around Loch Goil and then on up Loch Long to Arrochar, where the passengers disembarked to walk the two miles across to Tarbet on Loch Lomond, where another steamer carried them down to the railhead at Balloch.

Along with the expansion of the tourist trade in the mid-nineteenth century came the building of many fine Victorian villas along the banks of Loch Goil, as the moneyed classes in Glasgow could afford to build holiday homes or install their families away from the city and come to Lochgoilhead at the weekends.

After the Ardgoil peninsula became the property of Glasgow Corporation in 1906, thousands of city dwellers travelled to Lochgoilhead to enjoy a few hours of fresh air. An annual summer event in the 1920s was the arrival of a steamer chartered by Sir Godfrey Collins, of the Glasgow publishing house, who treated all his workers and their families to a day trip. However, in the 1940s the steamers began to give way to the more economical motorships and increasing numbers of people took to travelling by road. The Greenock to Lochgoilhead daily mail service, run by the *Comet*, was by 1946 no longer considered to be economically viable and in 1965 Lochgoilhead Pier closed following the final visit of the pleasure cruiser the *Maid of Skelmorlie*.

The earliest parts of the castle at Carrick, which was built by the Campbells of Loch Awe, date from the late fourteenth century, although it is probable that an earlier stronghold of the Lamonts was on the same site. The name is first recorded in 1428, when a legal summons was served on Duncan Campbell at 'le Carryk', and in 1529 Archibald, fourth Earl of Argyll, granted the 'castle and fortalice' in liferent to successive countesses. Mary, Queen of Scots, spent a night at the castle in 1563 when she was on her way to Inveraray – it was an important staging post between the Clyde and Loch Fyne. From the late fifteenth century until 1685 Carrick Castle was held for the earls of Argyll by hereditary captains descended from the Campbells of Ardkinglas, the earliest of whom was Robert Campbell, whose name is first mentioned in 1494. The captain was required to maintain the castle and its attached lands (which stretched from Lettermay to Stronvochlan, near Ardentinny, and also included isolated properties in Glendaruel and Rosneath) at his own expense. In a bond of 1674 John Campbell undertook 'to make my actual residence and dwelling in the said Castle of Carrick alsoft as conveintlie I may', to perform the usual duties required, 'especiallie the resaving and keeping of prisoners', and to employ a porter and two nightwatchmen. Campbell was summoned to Edinburgh in 1685 to prevent his aiding the ninth Earl of Argyll, who was involved in a plot to depose James VII, and in May of that year the castle was destroyed on the orders of the Privy Council. No attempt was made to restore it and the Campbell family of Carrick died out in the mid-eighteenth century.

Carrick, like Lochgoilhead, was a small rural settlement in the nineteenth century, with sheep and the fishing trade providing its inhabitants with their principal subsistence. Carrick Pier opened in 1877 to accommodate the steamers and some Victorian villas were subsequently built along the shore road. Until the 1930s, however, the road from Lochgoilhead ran only as far as Douglas Pier.

The communities around Loch Goil, like many other small villages, were deeply affected by the two world wars. Sixteen young men were killed in the Great War and four between 1939 and 1945. Dozens more were involved in the services or toiled on the Home Front. Several families were evacuated to the area during the Glasgow blitz and a number of householders billeted servicemen, many of whom were convalescing. A naval base was set up at Douglas Pier, since the Admiralty needed to measure the underwater noise made by a submarine, and Loch Goil proved to be the ideal location, both for its quietness and depth and for its proximity to the depot facilities in the Clyde. As well as the submarines, many merchant ships moored in the loch, waiting for a suitable time to cross the Atlantic. The base was retained and expanded after the war, though the naval personnel were replaced by a civilian staff.

Loch Goil in the twenty-first century is still a favoured holiday destination. Several of the large Victorian villas, particularly those on the east side of the loch, remain as holiday homes, and a number of Glasgow people own caravans or chalets on the Drimsynie Estate and escape from the city at weekends. There are two outdoor education centres, offering such activities as sailing, canoeing and rock-climbing, which host large numbers of children annually. Although the vast majority of people arrive nowadays by car rather than by steamer, they continue to enjoy the beauty of this little corner of Argyll.

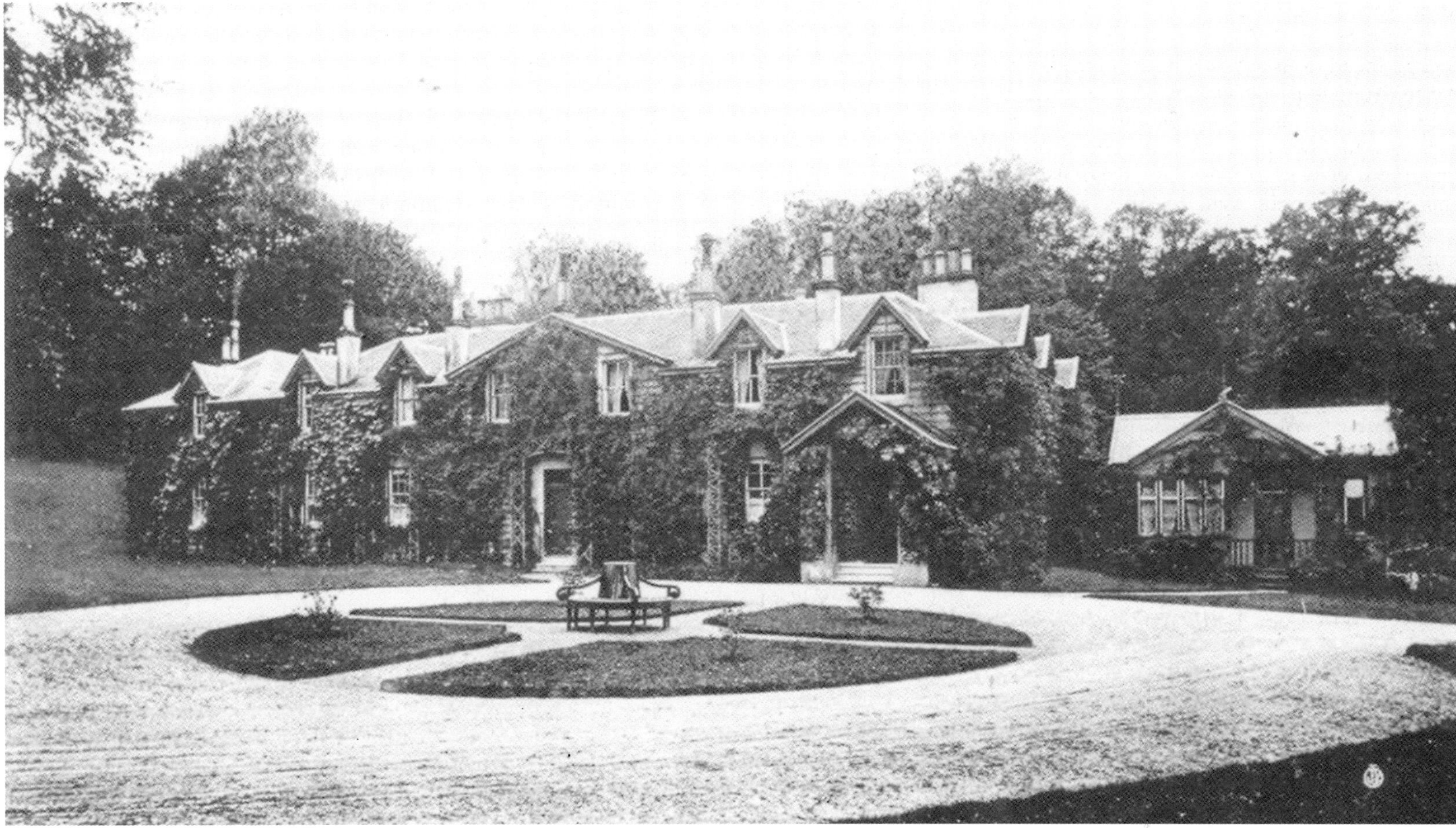

Until 1905 much of Lochgoilhead belonged to the Ardkinglas Estate, originally part of the Duke of Argyll's lands that stretched as far as Dumbarton. In 1831 the main house, owned by James Callendar of Ardkinglas, was destroyed by fire 'as the tradesmen were just finishing extensive repairs it had undergone'. The 'Old House', shown in this 1905 photo, which had been stables and accommodation for coachmen and servants, was then converted for the family and the Callendars lived here until the estate was sold. It is thought that the architect Robert Lorimer may have done some work on the building when he designed the present Ardkinglas House (1906–8) for Sir Andrew Noble, who purchased the estate in 1905. The Old House gradually fell into disrepair and was finally demolished in the 1930s, although some foundations and walls are still visible. The corrugated iron summer house on the right of the picture was dismantled and given to the Luke family of Rosemary Cottage, Laglingartan, to help house their large family!

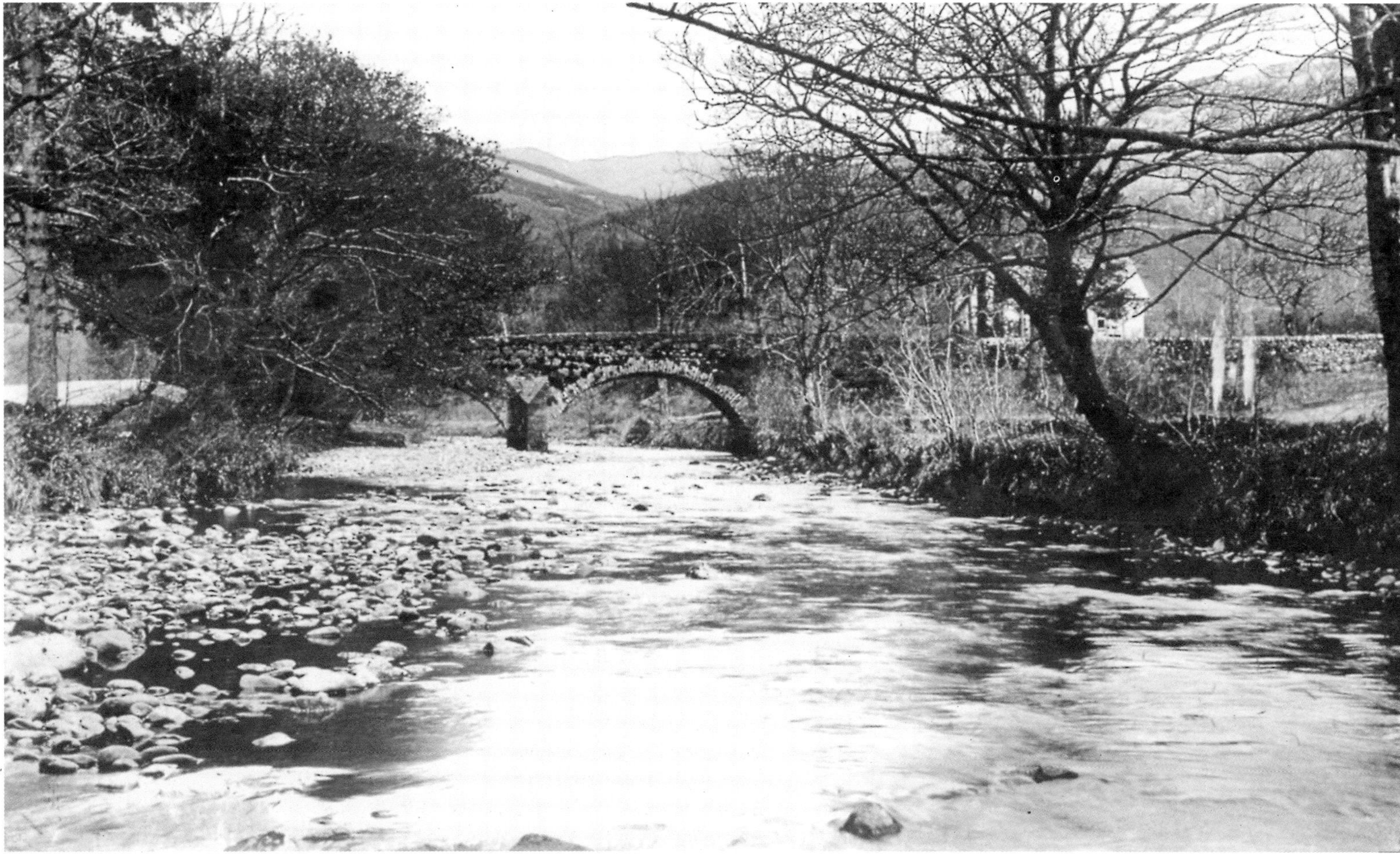

This late 1920s photo shows the last of the three bridges over the River Goil on the way into Lochgoilhead. It is not known when this bridge was built, but the Hell's Glen bridge dates from 1810 and is listed. Before roads and bridges were adopted by councils and central government, the cost and the labour for repairs had to be provided by the local inhabitants. The *Statistical Account* observes: 'It is found very difficult to keep up the bridges ... the rivers swell so suddenly, and rush down from the mountains with such rapidity, that the bridges must be built in very advantageous situations, in order to stand any time. There is one bridge in particular, near Lochgoil-head, which has fallen down three times, within the last 15 years; it was built at first, and twice rebuilt, at the expence of the inhabitants.'

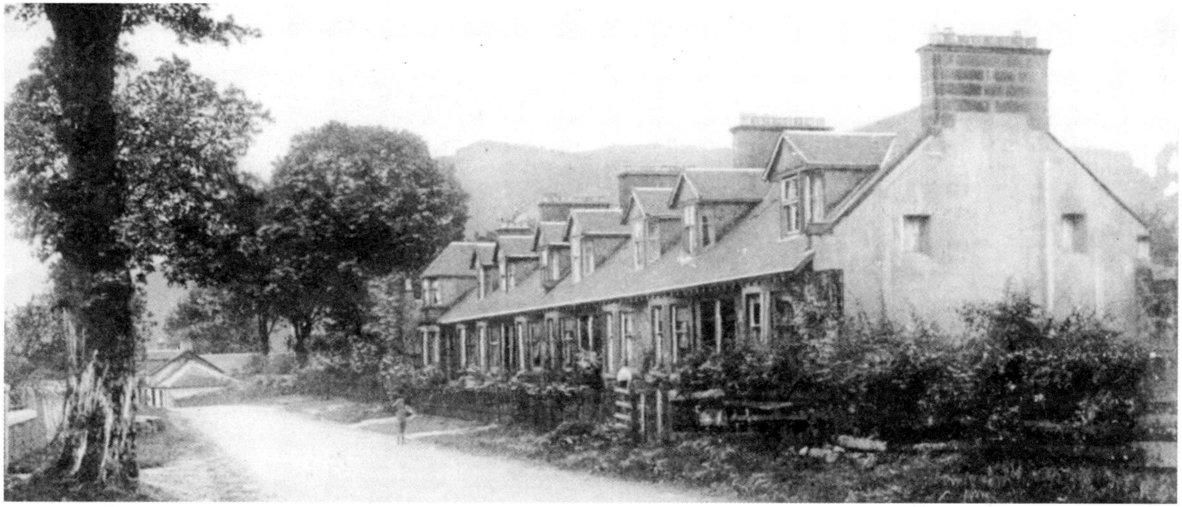

Viewfield Terrace, c.1905. It is thought that the terrace was possibly built initially to accommodate the artisans or tradesmen working on the Glasgow merchants' villas up the side of the loch. The two fireplaces visible on the gable end suggest that the original intention was to continue the terrace.

Ben Arthur Place, seen here on a postcard from the early 1920s, was one of the first groups of houses to be built on glebe land in the 1880s. The house furthest away is 'Parkview', built in 1884 by local builder and joiner Donald McKellar at a cost of £2000 for Mrs Eliza Craig Smith, wife of the schoolmaster William Smith. Later occupants of 'Parkview' included the proprietor of the hotel, a local bus driver, and a retired naval officer.

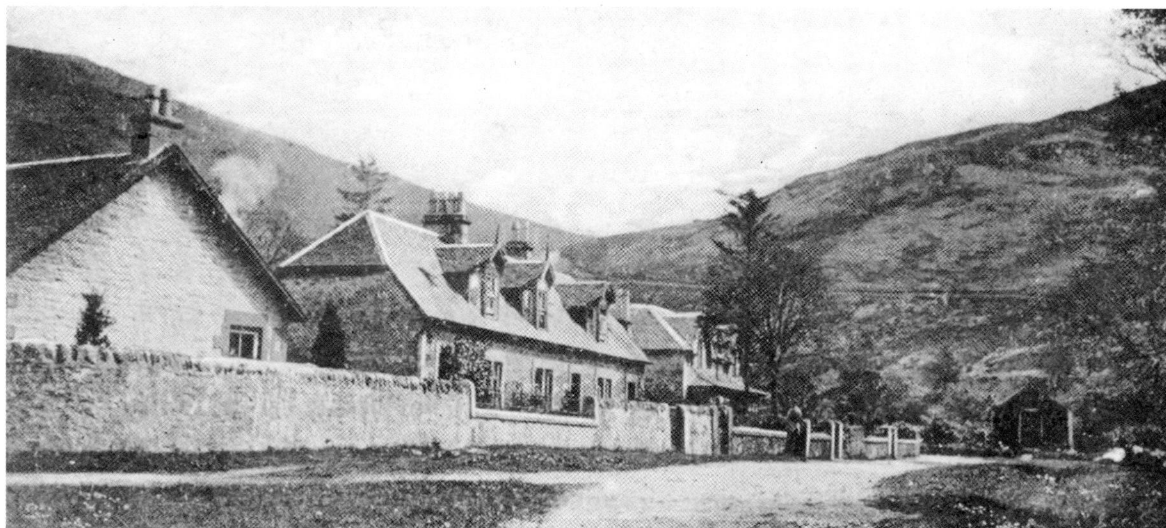

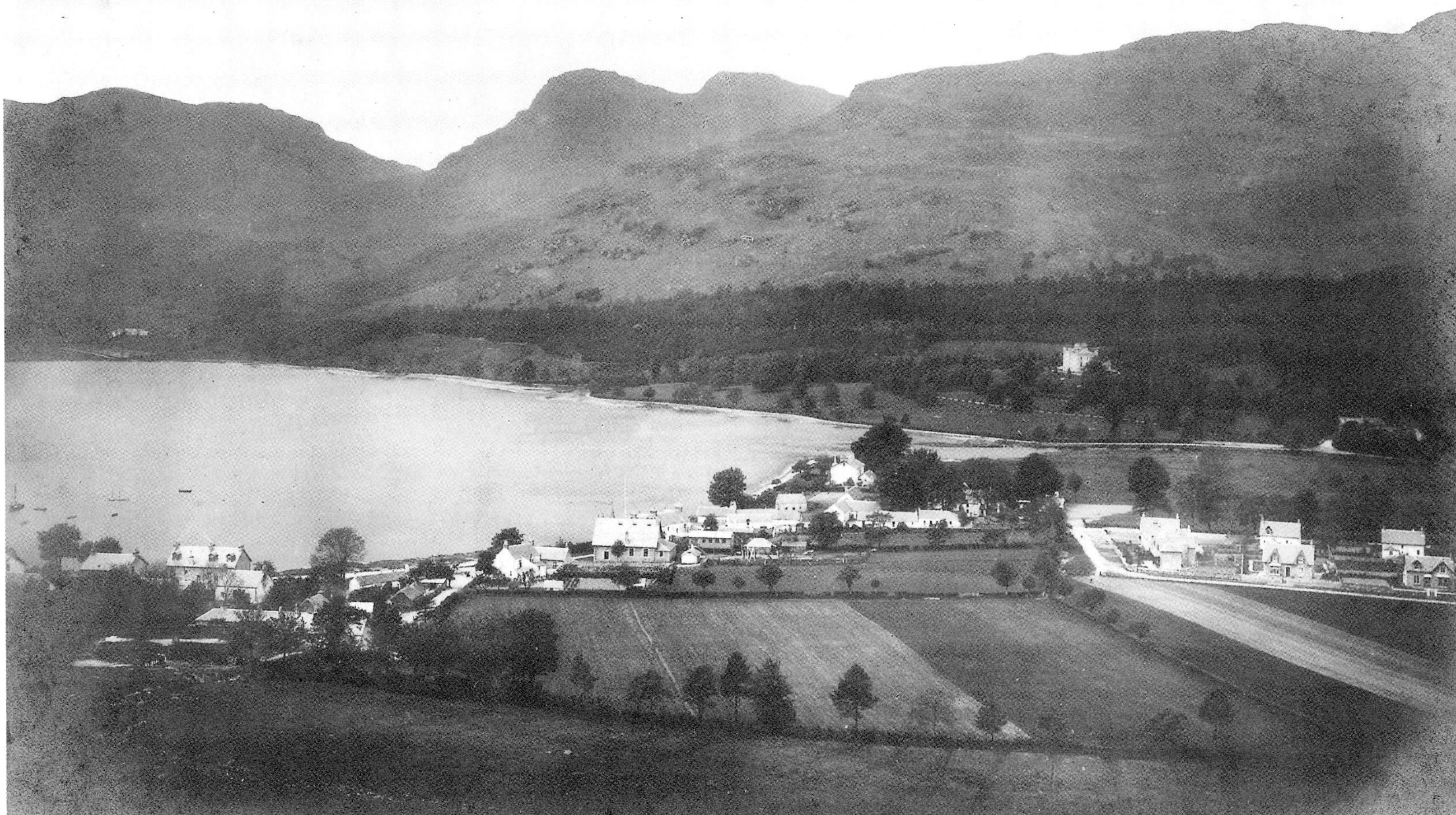

A photograph from about 1886 of Lochgoilhead from the north-east shows the village before its expansion and infilling and is taken before the building of Viewfield Terrace, the shelter park and the village hall. In the middle distance thatched weavers' cottages can just be made out and there is a building in front of Lochgoilhead Farm. This may possibly have been an earlier school building.

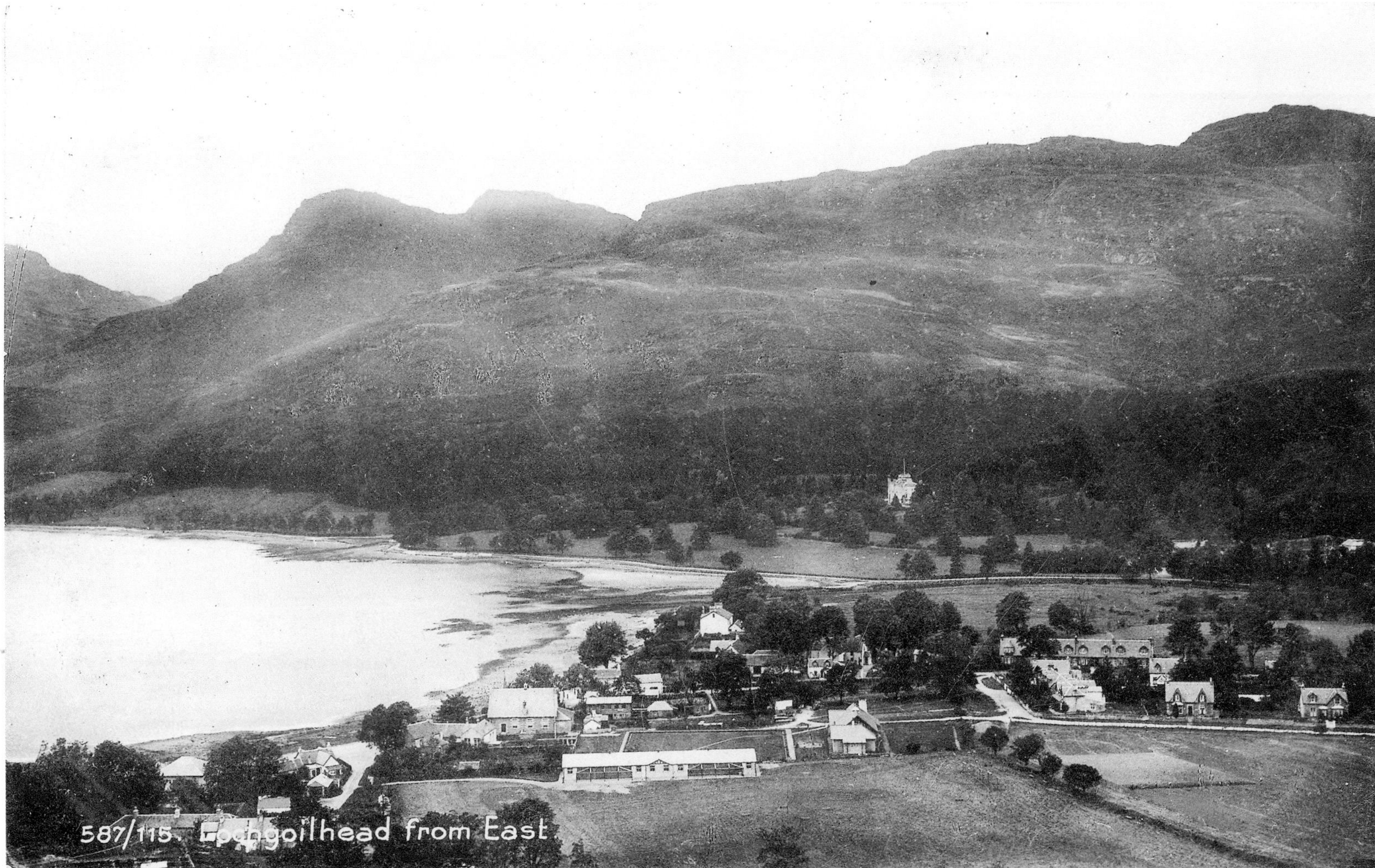

A few years later (c.1901) the shelter park is visible in the foreground and the village hall has been built (1898, designed by James Salmon). Viewfield Terrace has appeared behind the villas on the right. The weavers' cottages and the 'school building' have gone.

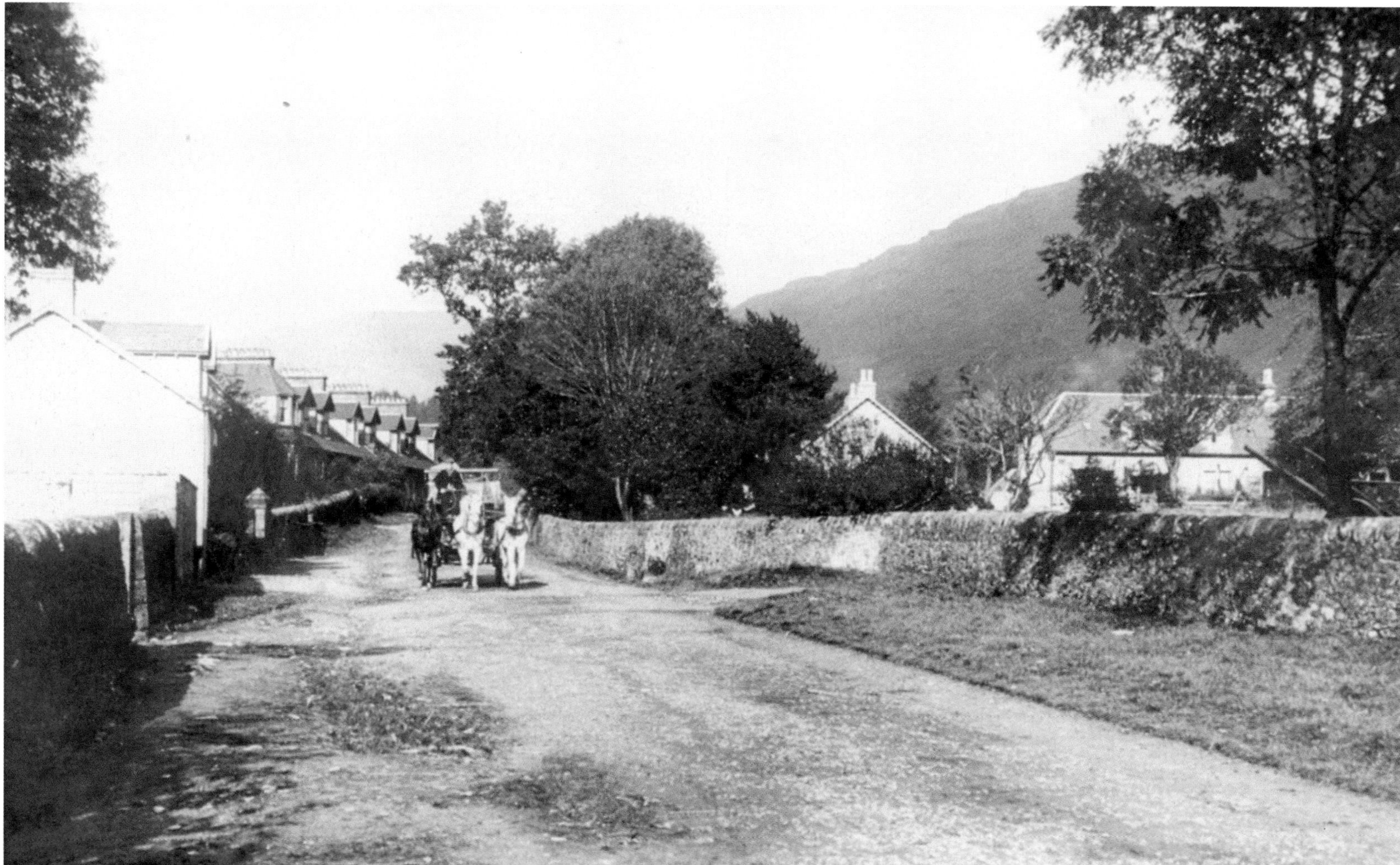

The coach from St. Catherine's to Lochgoilhead passing Viewfield Terrace, c.1905, with Ben Arthur Place on the right and heading towards the shore. The coachman might be Hugh Cameron, who took over the run from his father (1826–1903) of the same name. They lived at Monevechadan, and were both known as 'Hughie the Coach'. The coachmen used to regale their passengers with ghost stories as they passed through Hell's Glen, although nothing terrible of any note had ever happened in Hell's Glen at this time.

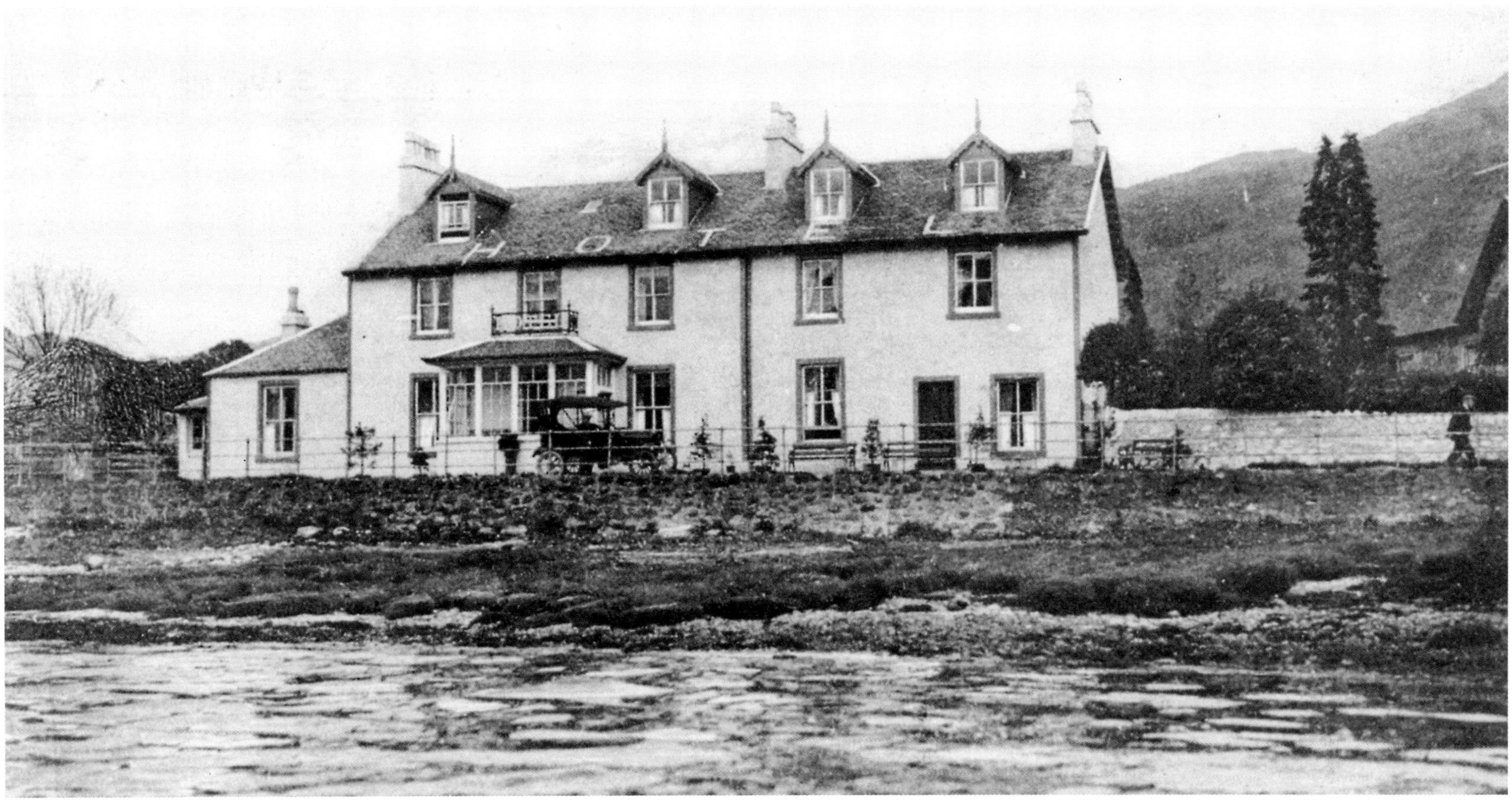

The main part of Lochgoilhead Hotel, seen here in the 1920s, dates from the eighteenth century, but is probably on the site of an earlier inn dating from the seventeenth century. Murray's 1875 *Handbook for Travellers* describes the hotel as 'a comfortable inn, surpassed by few for beauty of situation and fine scenery'. The Rev. Dugal McDougal, who compiled the *Statistical Account* in 1791, commented that the inn was necessary 'for the accommodation of the public … Lochgoilhead being a much frequented pass, especially in summer, between the West Highlands and the Low Country.' He remarked that, although spirits were sold on the premises, 'these, however, have no bad effects upon the morals of the inhabitants of this country'. Elsewhere the villagers are described as 'remarkable for their strict honesty, the regularity of their manners, their humanity and their courtesy to strangers'.

Ward Lock's *Pictorial and Descriptive Guide to Glasgow and the Clyde* gives the tariff for the hotel in 1930 as: 7/6 for bed and breakfast, 3/6 for lunch, 1/3 for tea and 5/- for dinner. The cost of bed and board was 12/- per day, £1 per weekend and 4 guineas per week.

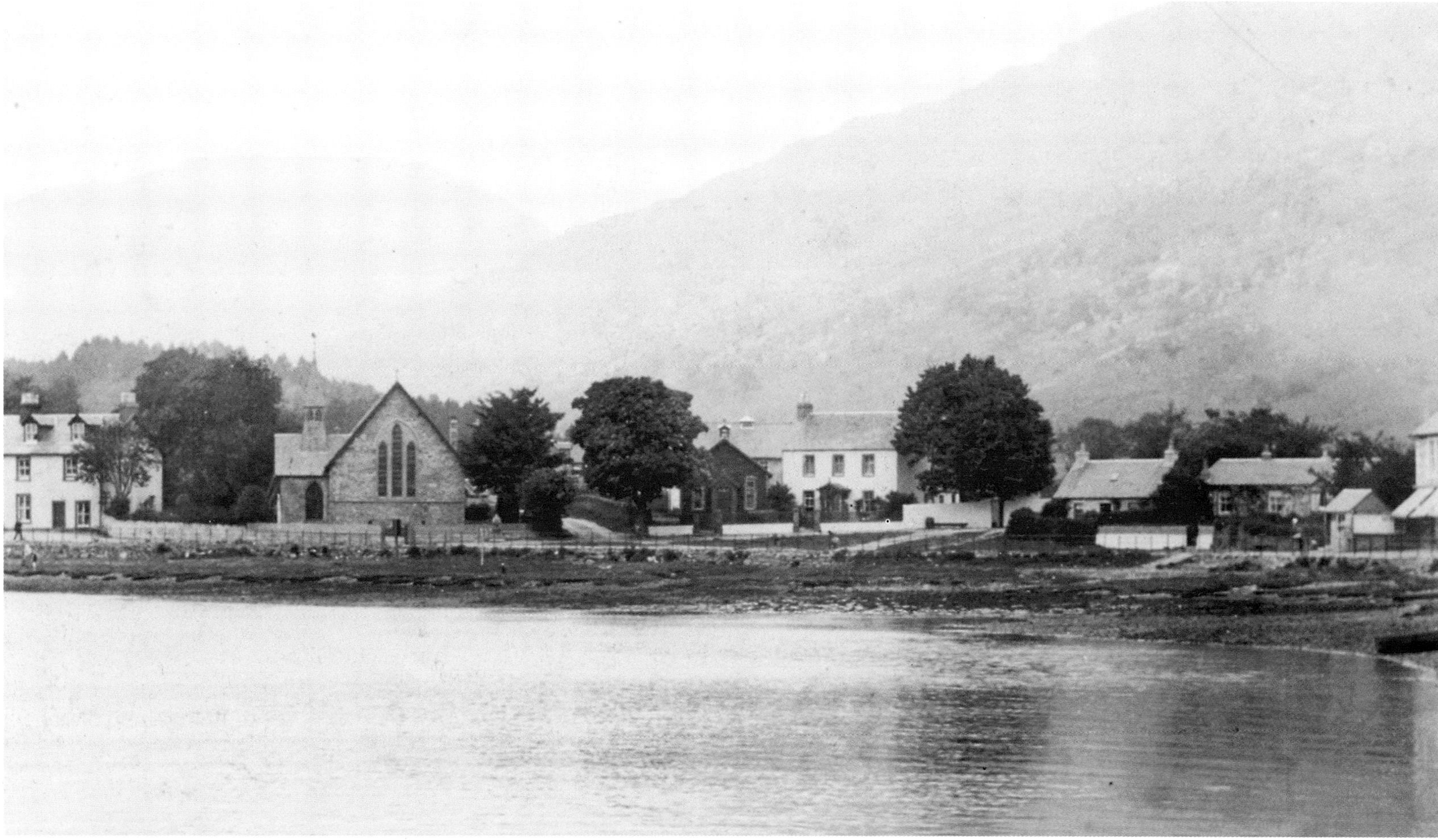

The United Free Church (usually known as the Gibson Church, after its first minister) on the left of this 1905 picture was built in 1883 to a design by the firm of Campbell Douglas and Sellars. Campbell Douglas lived in the village at Lochwood Villa in the 1880s. Although the United Free Church and the Church of Scotland were reunited in 1929, the Gibson Church retained its separate identity until 1952. At that point the parish church became the sole place of worship. The Gibson Church was used for a number of years after as the church hall. Its condition later deteriorated and it was demolished in 2002. Fortunately, one of the beautiful stained-glass windows was saved and plans are in hand to display this in the village hall, which can be seen through the trees to the right of the church.

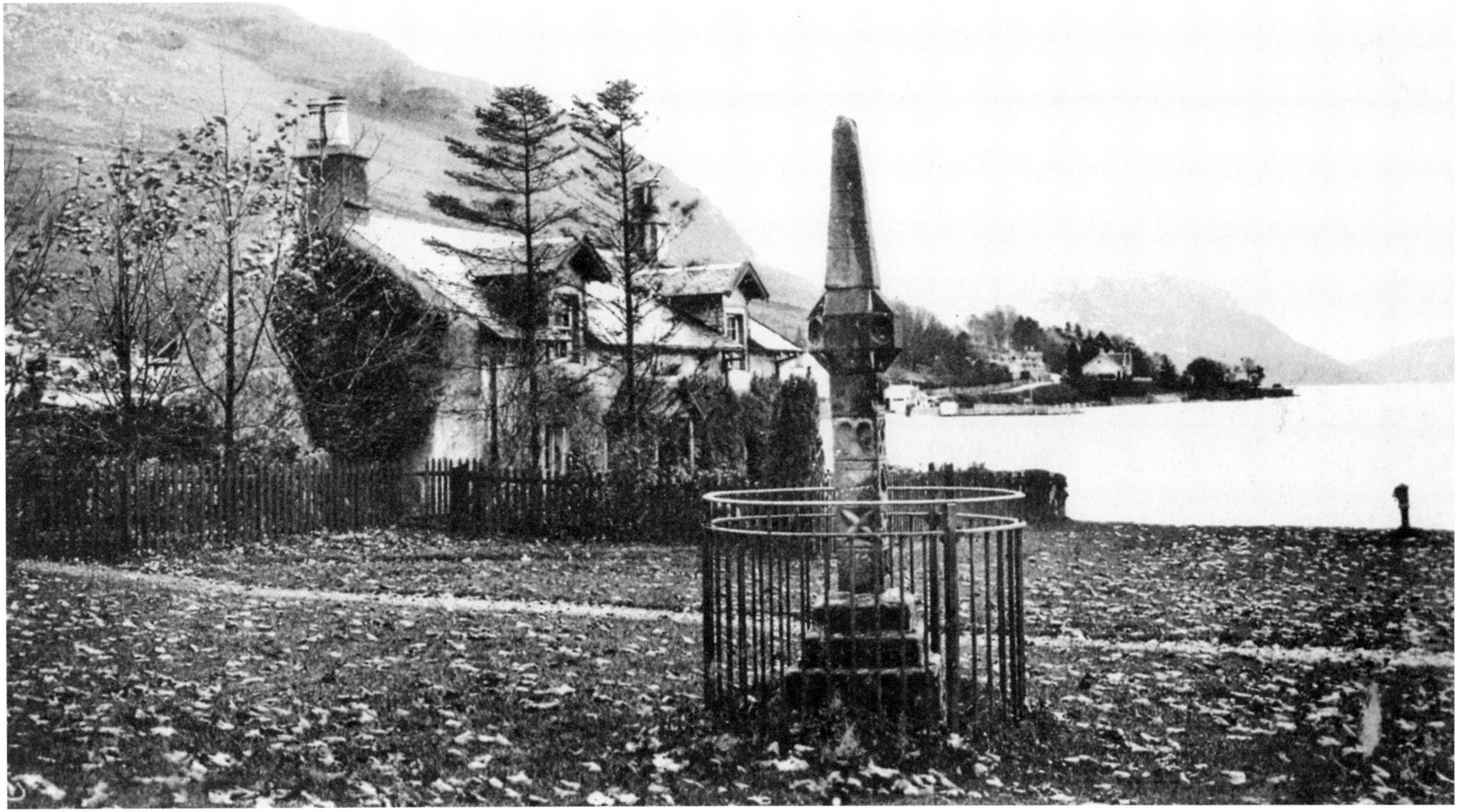

This 1904 postcard shows the sundial in front of Lochgoilhead Farm (now The Cottage), at the head of the loch. The house in the background is Lochview and a water pump can just be made out to the right. The sundial, which was probably originally in the grounds of Drimsynie House, was erected in 1626 to celebrate the marriage of Sir Colin Campbell, eighth Laird of Ardkinglas, and Helen Maxwell.

Sir Colin had been saved from a capsized galley off Strone Point after the sacking of Rathlin Island (off the Antrim Coast) in 1615, in a wreck that claimed the life of his father. In 1618 he was 'charged with the custody of the King's Peace in Cowall' (meaning he was to keep law and order) and in 1622 he was commissioned by the Privy Council to pursue the Clan Cameron 'with fire and sword'.

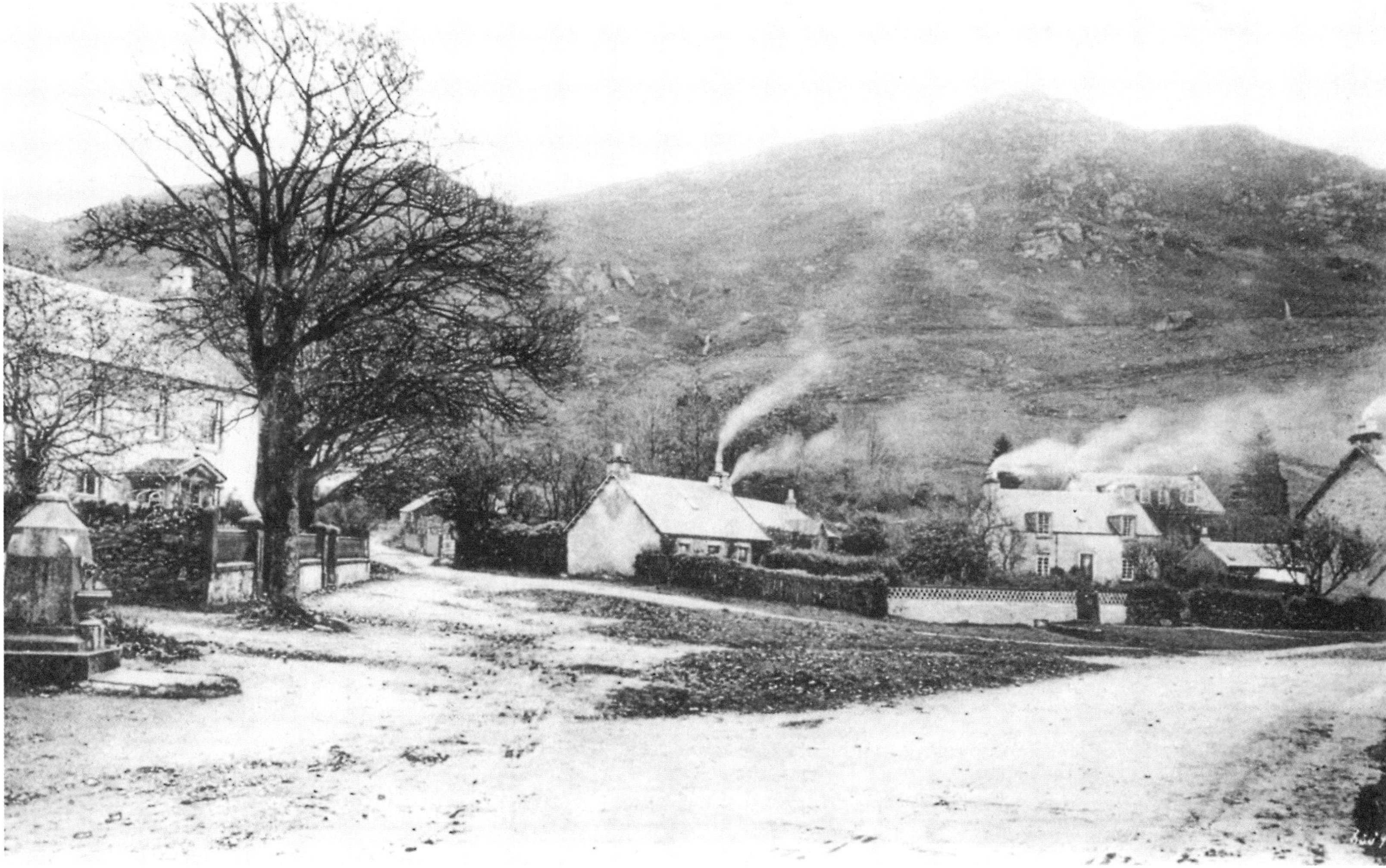

This picture was almost certainly taken on the same day as the previous image. Behind the fountain (on the very left) is the school house, in the centre of the picture is Callander Cottage, and to the right Burnside. The water fountain was erected in 1882 in memory of Neil Campbell, who was born in Lochgoilhead in 1837 and served for several years as merchant and postmaster. When he died suddenly, in September 1879, a lengthy obituary was published in the *Dunoon Herald*, which stated that 'a mournful gloom' had fallen over the village.

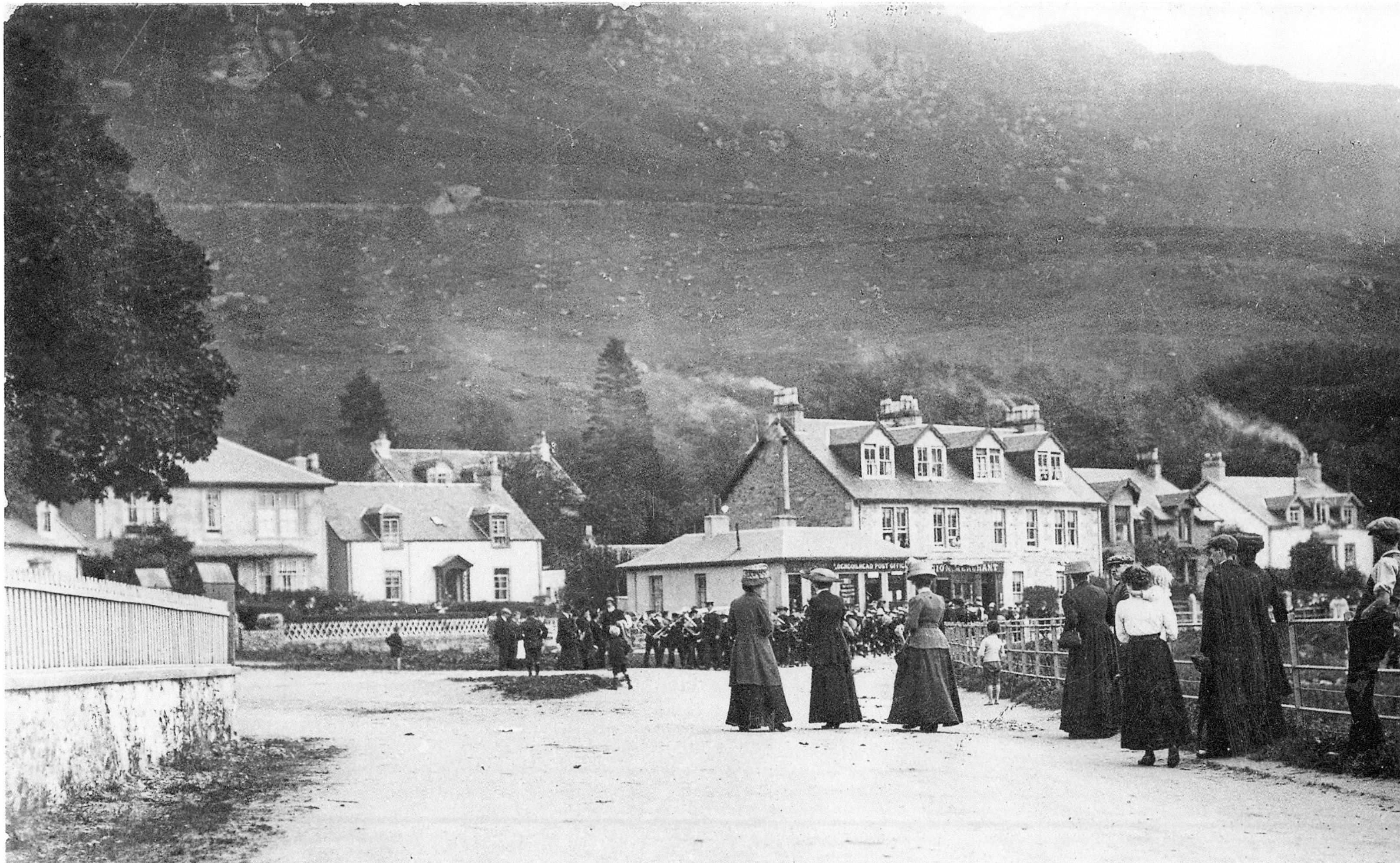

The little building (in the centre of the picture) was constructed early in the 1900s for Mrs Haggart, who ran the Post Office there from 1908 until 1946. It also housed the manual telephone exchange. The office had to be manned twenty-four hours a day in order for the postmistress to accept incoming telegrams and telephone calls. Telegrams had to be handwritten and were then delivered by bicycle – on the occasion of a wedding as many as a hundred telegrams might be received and villagers would be employed to help deliver them.

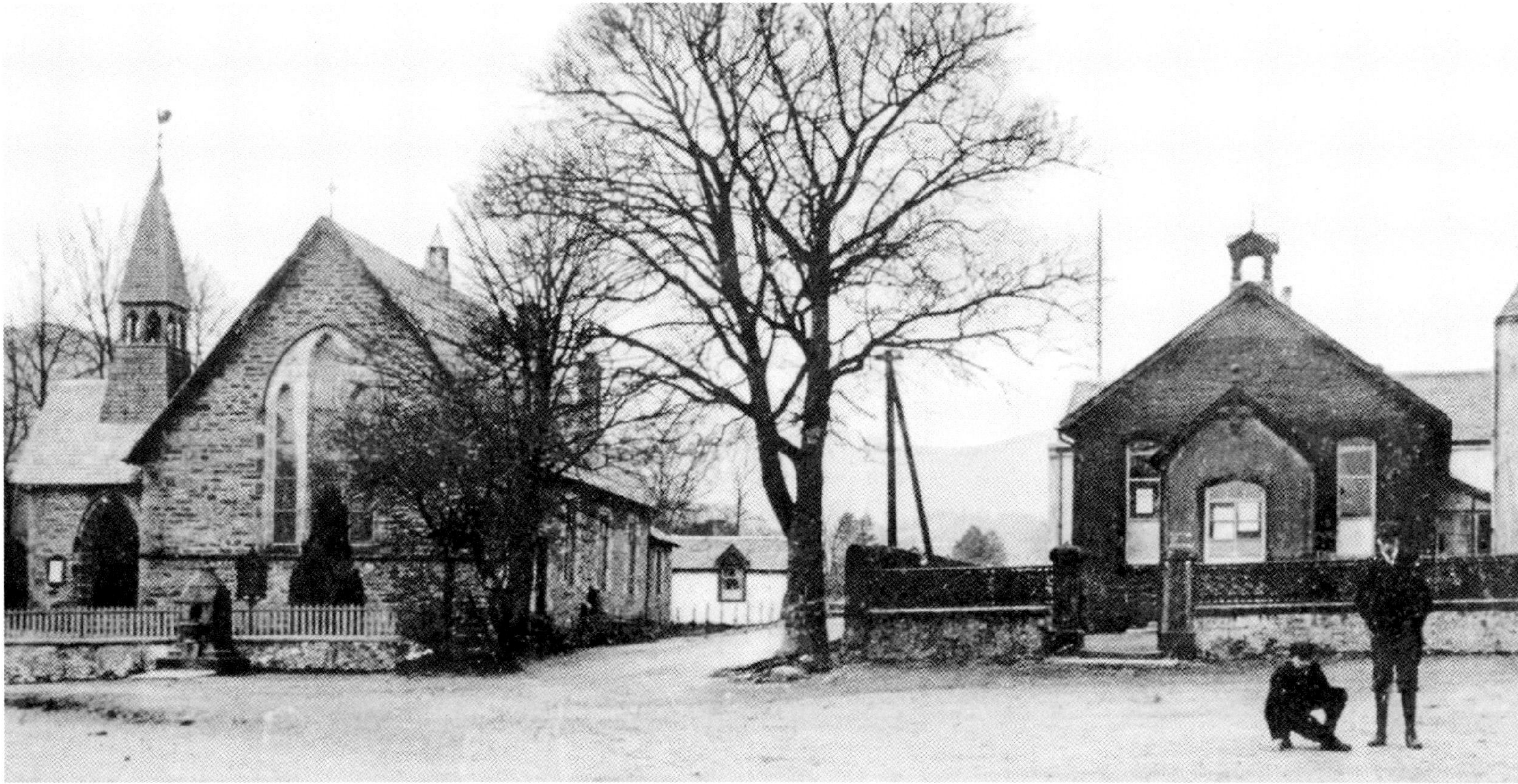

On the right is the old school house, which was built in 1877 and demolished in the early 1980s. Its replacement, opened in 1962, is in Hall Road, which runs between the old school and the former United Free Church (on the left). In the 1870s and 1880s the school was under the control of the infamous William Smith, who administered castor oil to his pupils as a punishment. A newspaper reporter from Glasgow wrote about him, which resulted in a government inspector visiting the school. Questions were asked in Parliament and 'Castor Oil' Smith was eventually dismissed.

According to the *Statistical Account*, in the 1790s about forty children attended the parochial school and about sixty went to the school at Cairndow. Pupils learnt 'Latin, English, Gaelic, writing, arithmetic, book-keeping, navigation and church music'. At that time, although most people spoke English, Gaelic was the predominant language. Even at the time of the 1891 census, with the influx of 'second home' owners, 235 people, about half the population of the village, were listed as speaking Gaelic as well as English. In 1900 the school had thirty-six pupils. At that time few local children went on to further education, and most left when they were fourteen, the girls usually going into domestic service and the boys to work on the land.

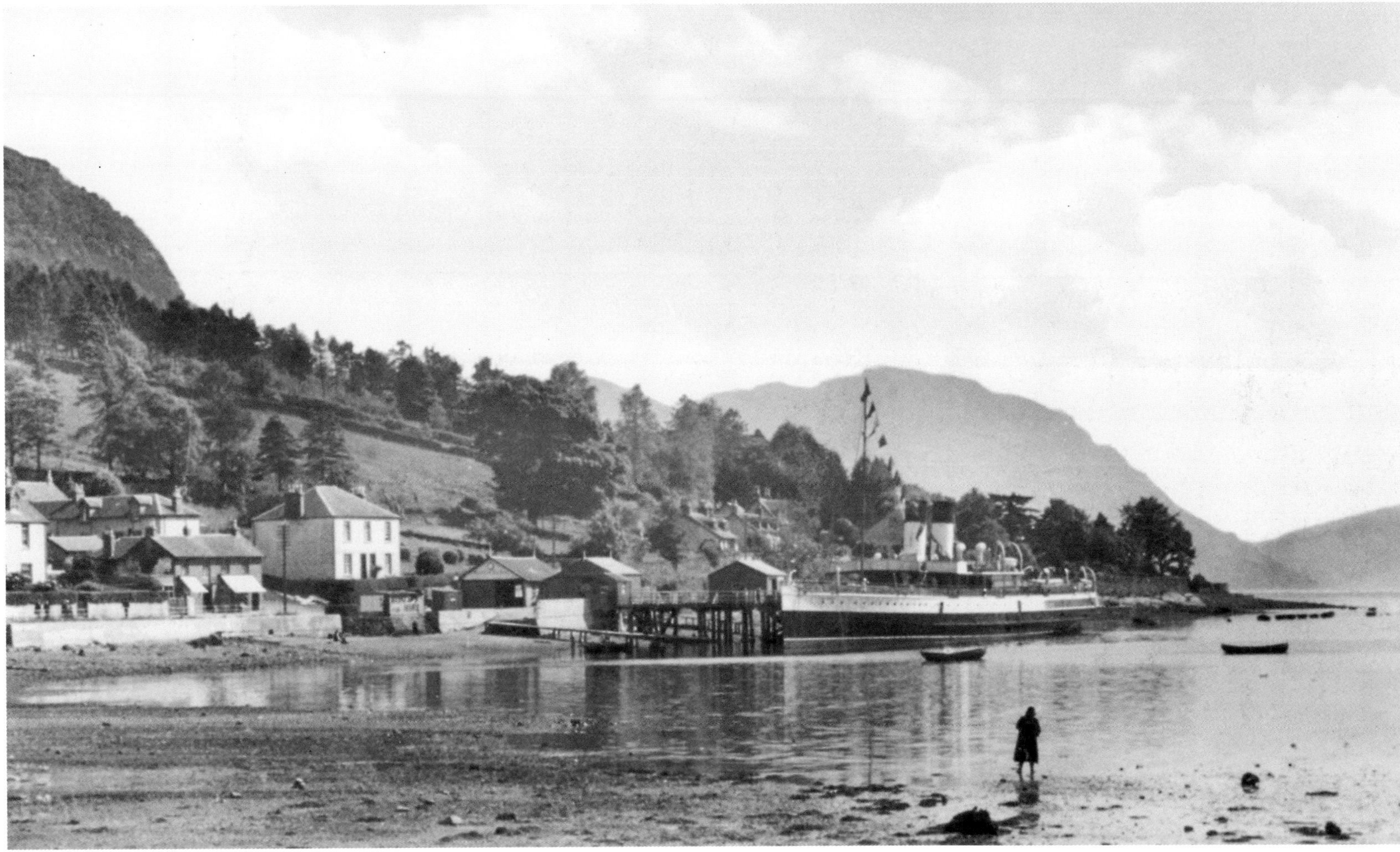

The revolutionary *King Edward*, built in 1901 for service on the Clyde, was the world's first steam turbine-powered passenger ship, using a form of propulsion first demonstrated by the engineer Charles Parsons on the launch *Turbinia* in 1896. A more efficient user of steam, the turbine was to replace the reciprocating engine as the main power source for screw steamers, and the speed and economy of the *King Edward* soon made the turbine the chosen method of propulsion for Clyde steamers on the long-haul cruise routes to Campbeltown and Inveraray. Seen here at the pier in the late 1930s, the *King Edward* was one of the steamers hired by Glasgow Corporation during the 1937 coronation celebrations to bring families to Loch Goil for the day.

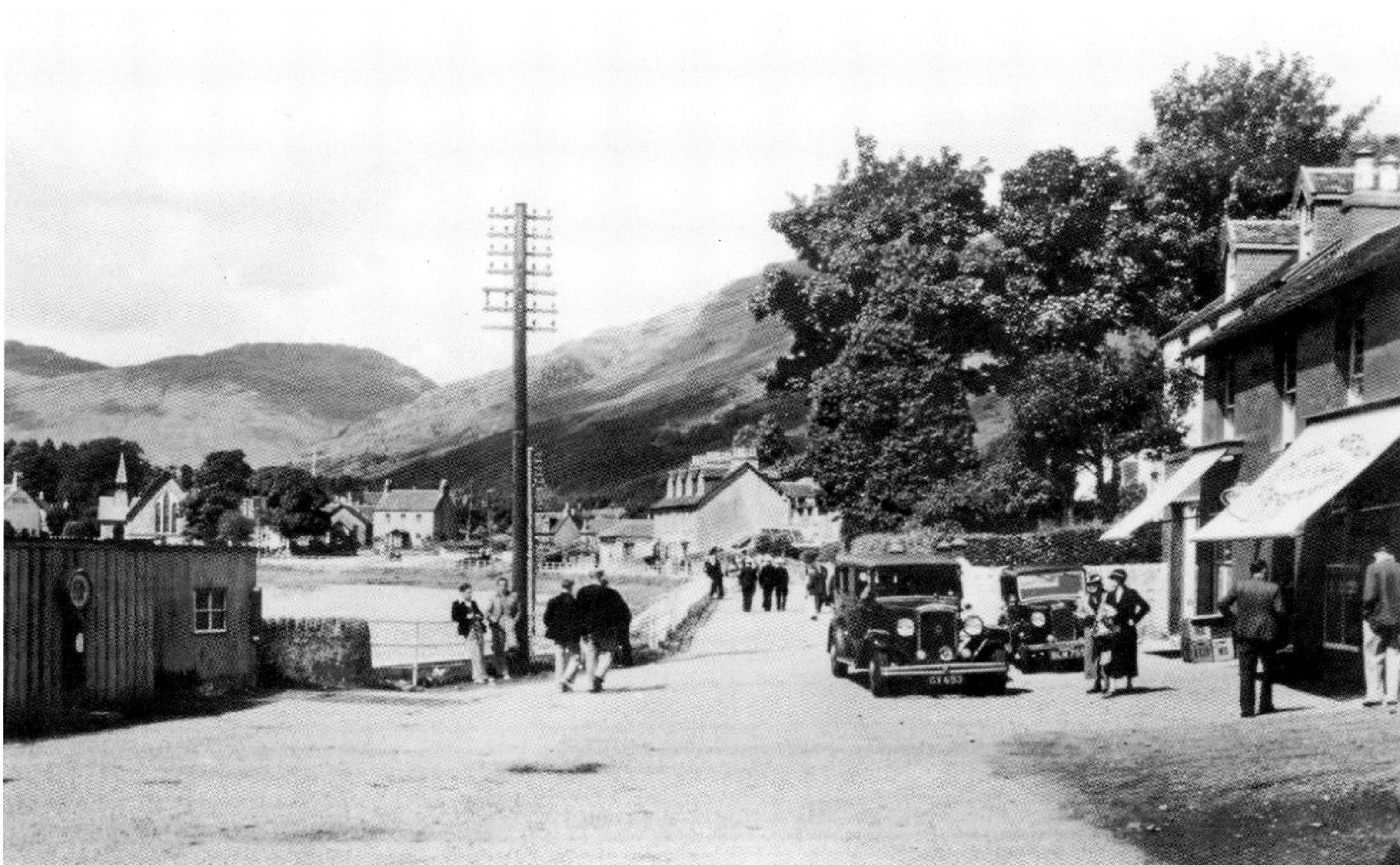

The age of the motor car was somewhat delayed in reaching the village properly. The journey by steamer from Glasgow took only two hours, little more than it takes by car today. Until the 1920s the Rest and Be Thankful needed to be ascended in reverse and an eight mile single-track road would, as now, deter some drivers. This late 1930s postcard view, however, with the pier head stores on the right, shows that those determined and rich enough were beginning to visit in their cars.

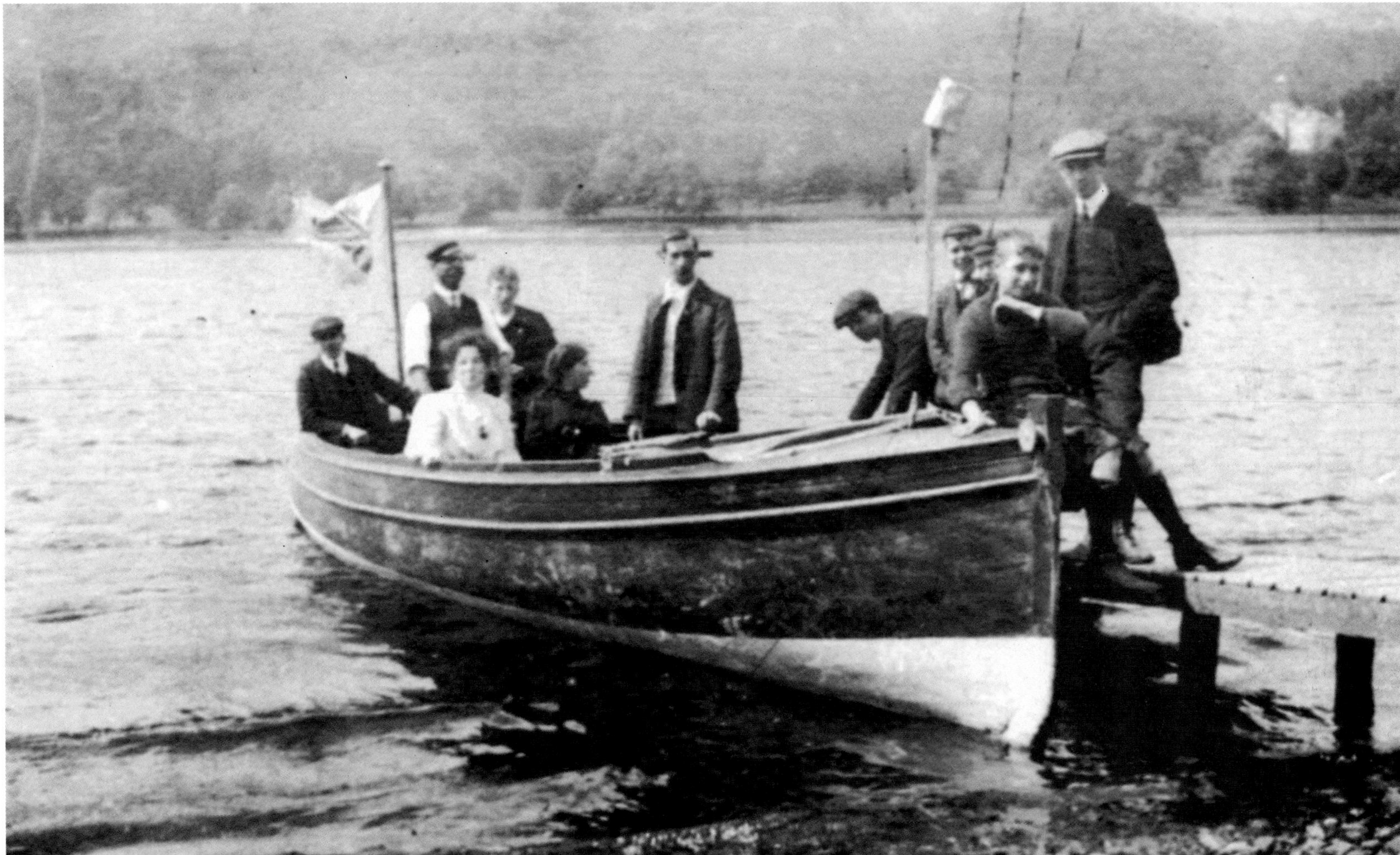

This private photograph, dated 1909, is probably of a tender from a private yacht or leisure boat. Such large vessels were not uncommon on the Clyde around this time. Before World War I the firth was the playground of the wealthy and it was estimated that there were more millionaires with homes on the Clyde than anywhere else in the country other than London.

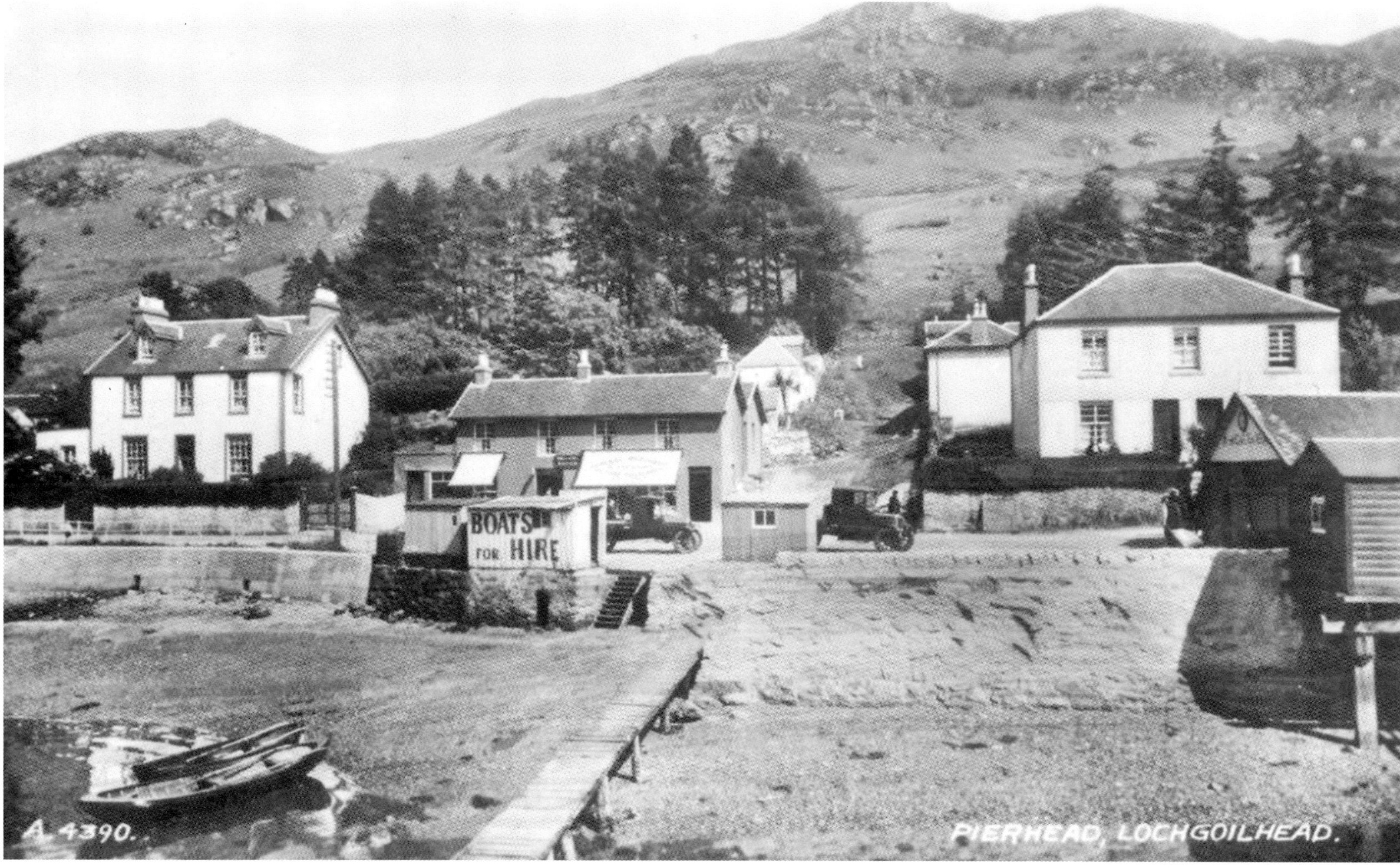


Behind the 'Boats for Hire' sign in this 1936 scene are the awnings for the pier head stores. The shop was known as Jackson's in the early part of the twentieth century, but by the 1930s it was run by Tom Cunningham and his wife Meg. In the early 1940s the shop had three separate areas. The main section was the grocery, the second part was the Post Office and the third part was closed, having formerly been a clothing store. At some point there had also been an operational bakehouse to the rear of the building.

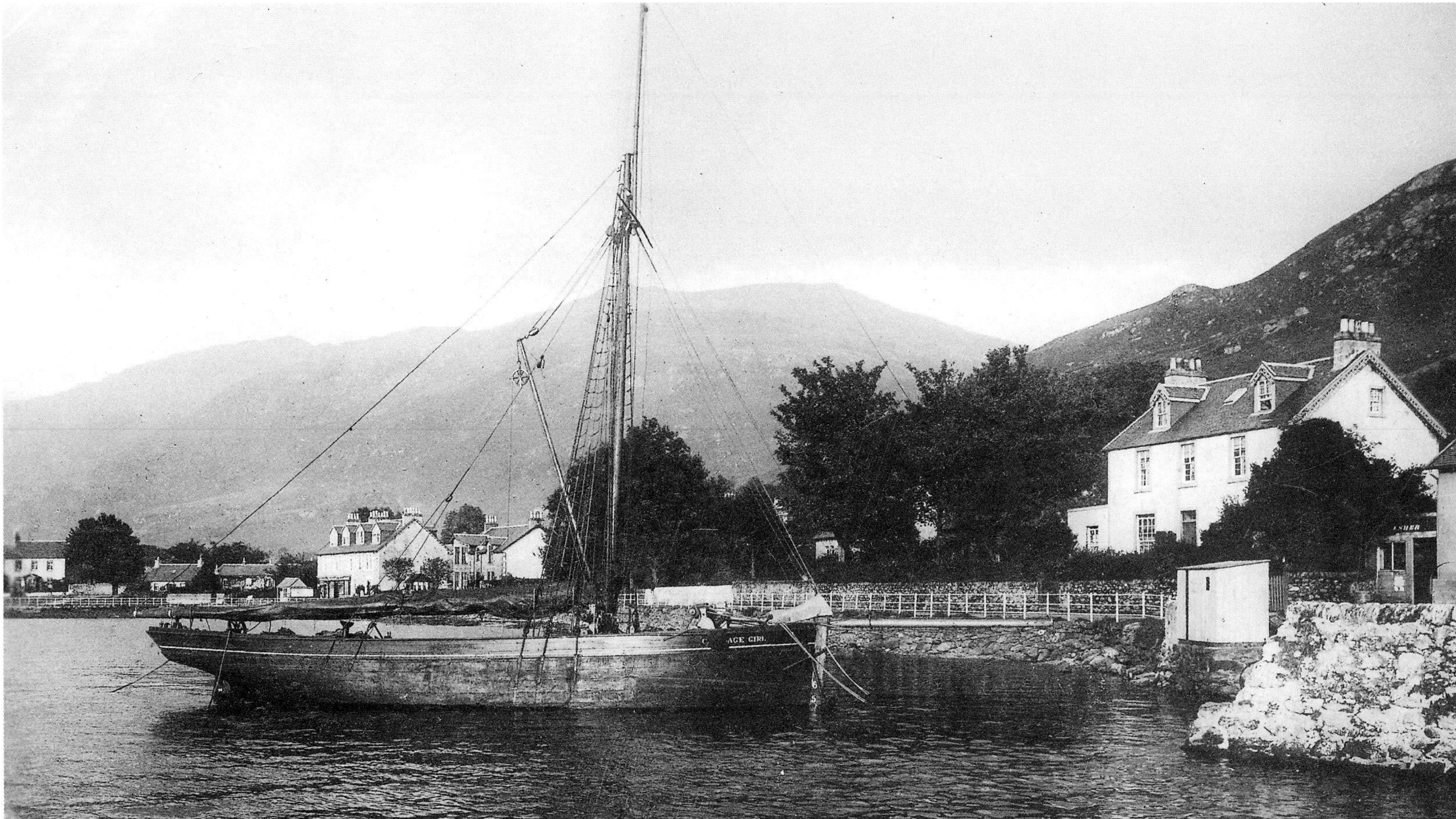

Gaff cutters, such as this unidentified one (*Girl* is the second half of the name) from about 1905 at Lochgoilhead Pier, plied their trade on the Clyde. This type of vessel may have continued to compete with steam puffers for comparatively small remote deliveries. Dan Mcdonald's book *The Steam Puffer* refers to such boats and says that some survived under sail into the 1930s. The photo shows a vessel of about 40 tons, which was most likely engaged in the supply of coal and building materials. On return trips she may have taken livestock and farm produce to market. Her angle suggests she is either settling on the bottom or in the process of floating off on the tide. Boats like this would have discharged their cargo into carts, using the derrick which is rigged up on the port side. This cutter was probably built in the second half of the nineteenth century and this one had seen a good bit of hard sailing, as evidenced by the strains (distortion of sheerline) on her chain plates.

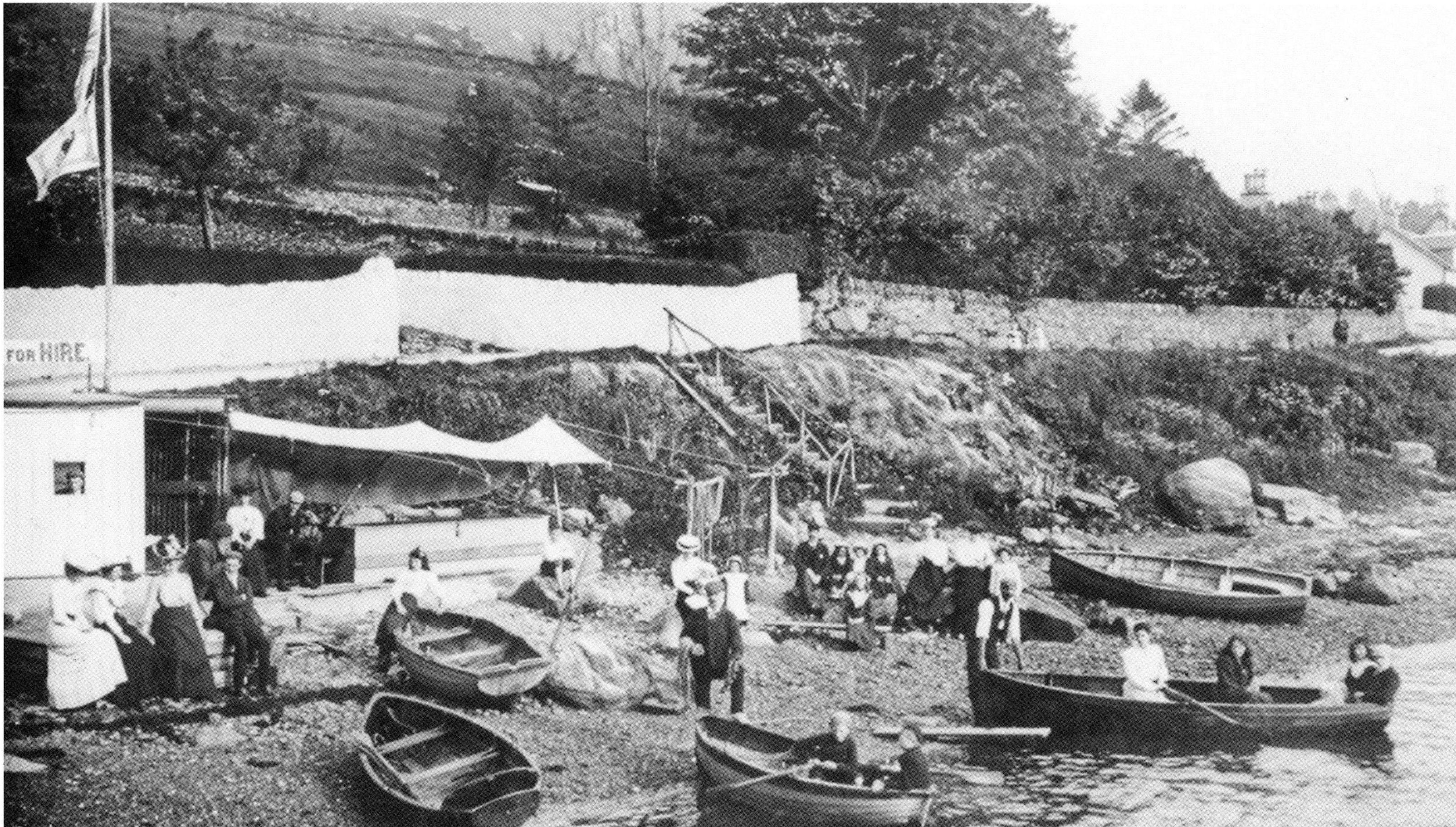


On the right of this picture, dating from c.1905, can be seen Planetree Cottage, which is where the McEwan family lived. The McEwans owned the pier and were also agents for MacBraynes; they effectively ran all aspects of the transport business, both freight and passengers. John McEwan, who died in 1895, was pier master for a number of years, and his four sons (Archibald, Donald, Alec and John) were also pier masters, at Lochgoilhead, Blairmore, Kilcreggan and Innellan. As they were all physically very alike, many a passenger wondered how the same pier master managed to be in several different locations at once!

Hiring a rowing boat was an integral part of a Clyde holiday or a day out. The availability of rowing boats declined in the 1970s, partly as a result of the introduction of health and safety regulations.

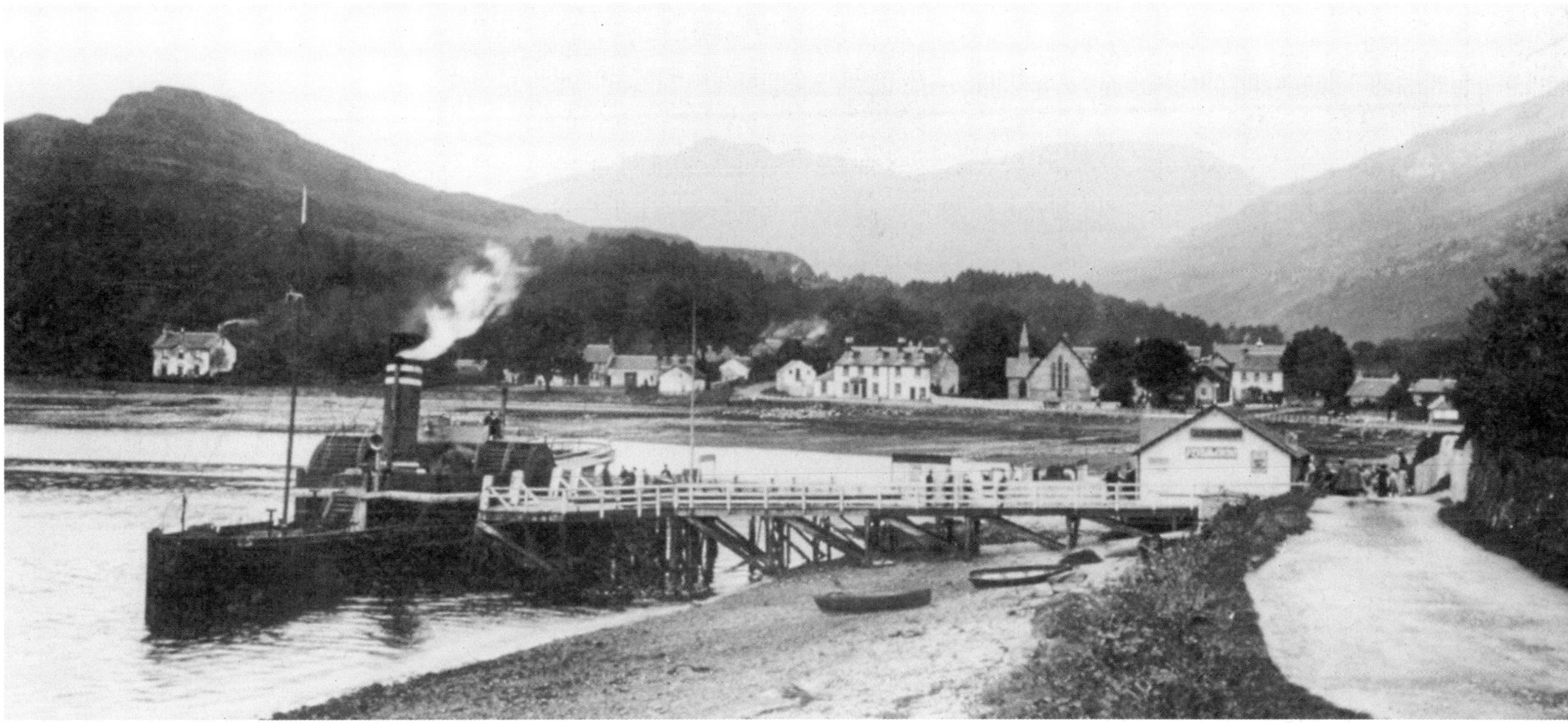

One of the oldest steamboat companies operating in the Clyde was the Loch Goil and Loch Long Steamboat Company, formed in 1825 to take advantage of the growing trade to Lochgoilhead as a route to Inveraray and Oban. New vessels were put on the service at regular intervals, culminating with their best-known steamer – *Edinburgh Castle*. The company won a considerable slice of the traffic bound for the county town of Inveraray. Although there were direct steamers from Glasgow, it was faster to take the boat to Lochgoilhead, transfer to a coach for the journey through Hell's Glen to St. Catherine's and then continue onward by ferry across Loch Fyne. Some passengers walked the eight miles between the two lochs.

In 1885 the Loch Goil and Loch Long Steamboat Company acquired the *Chancellor* from the Loch Lomond Steamboat Company, along with its Arrochar business. In 1909 it went into liquidation and its assets passed to the Lochgoil & Inveraray Steamboat Company, which also took over the Glasgow & Inveraray Steamboat Company. Their two main steamers were then sold in 1912 to Turbine Steamers Ltd., whose fast and modern turbine steamers had come to dominate the Inveraray excursion trade. The Loch Eck steamer *Fairy Queen* remained in the company's possession. In 1914 the *Comet* was brought into the Greenock–Lochgoilhead service, which continued for a further thirty years. Increasingly the improvements in road services and the popularity of the car signalled the demise of the age of the steamer and, for a time at least, Loch Goil became somewhat of a backwater. This photograph from c. 1905 shows the *Edinburgh Castle* at Lochgoilhead Pier. The original wooden jetty, built in 1825, was replaced in 1850 with a more substantial pier.

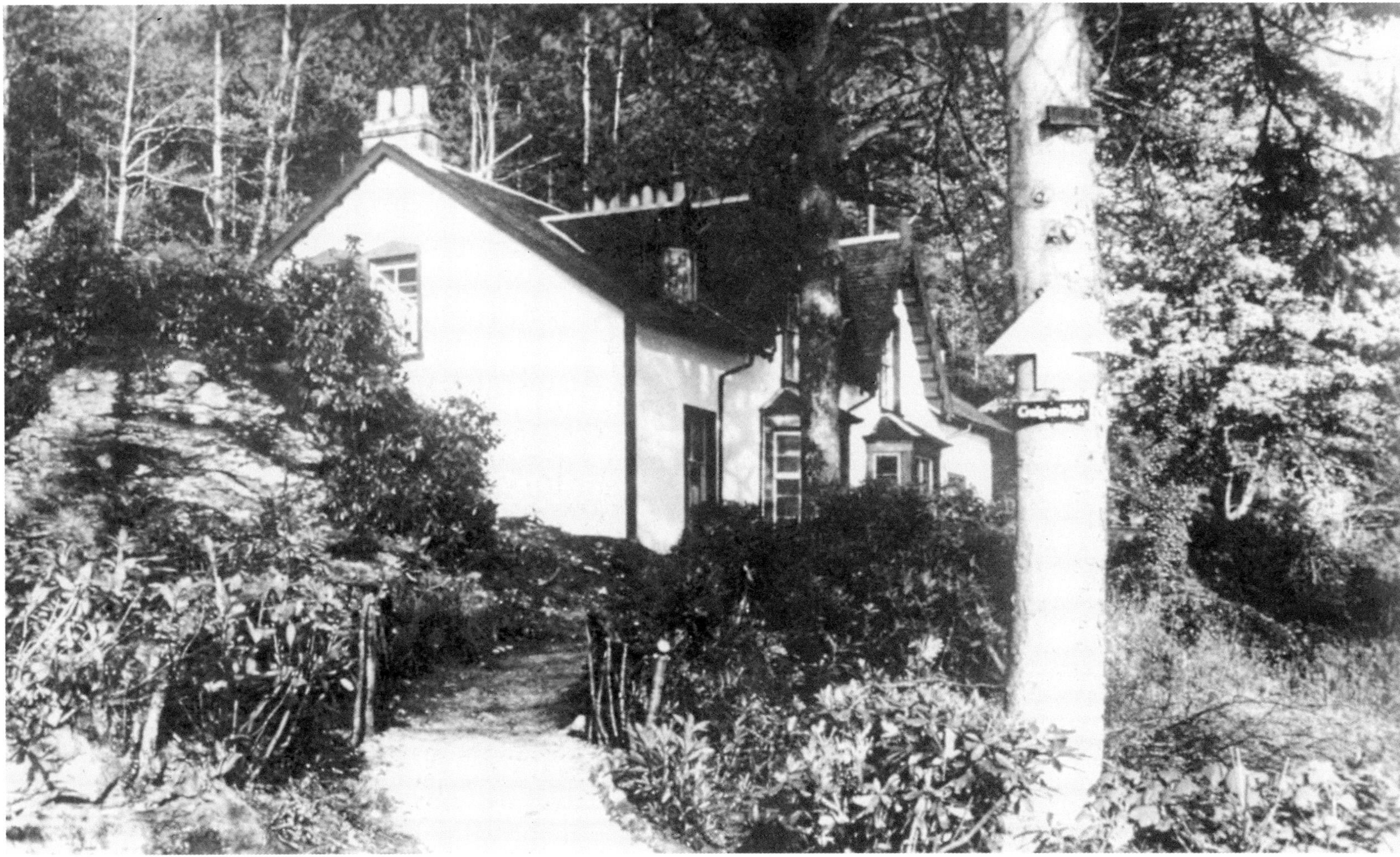

Craig-an-Righ (Rock of the King) was apparently built in the 1860s for a retired general. Later, along with the whole of the Ardgoil peninsula, it was donated to Glasgow Corporation, who owned it until the 1960s. When run by the SYHA the house is thought to have been a hostel for girls. A little further down the road Captain George Pound, a champion of the sea-scout movement, held camps in his garden at Inverlounin.

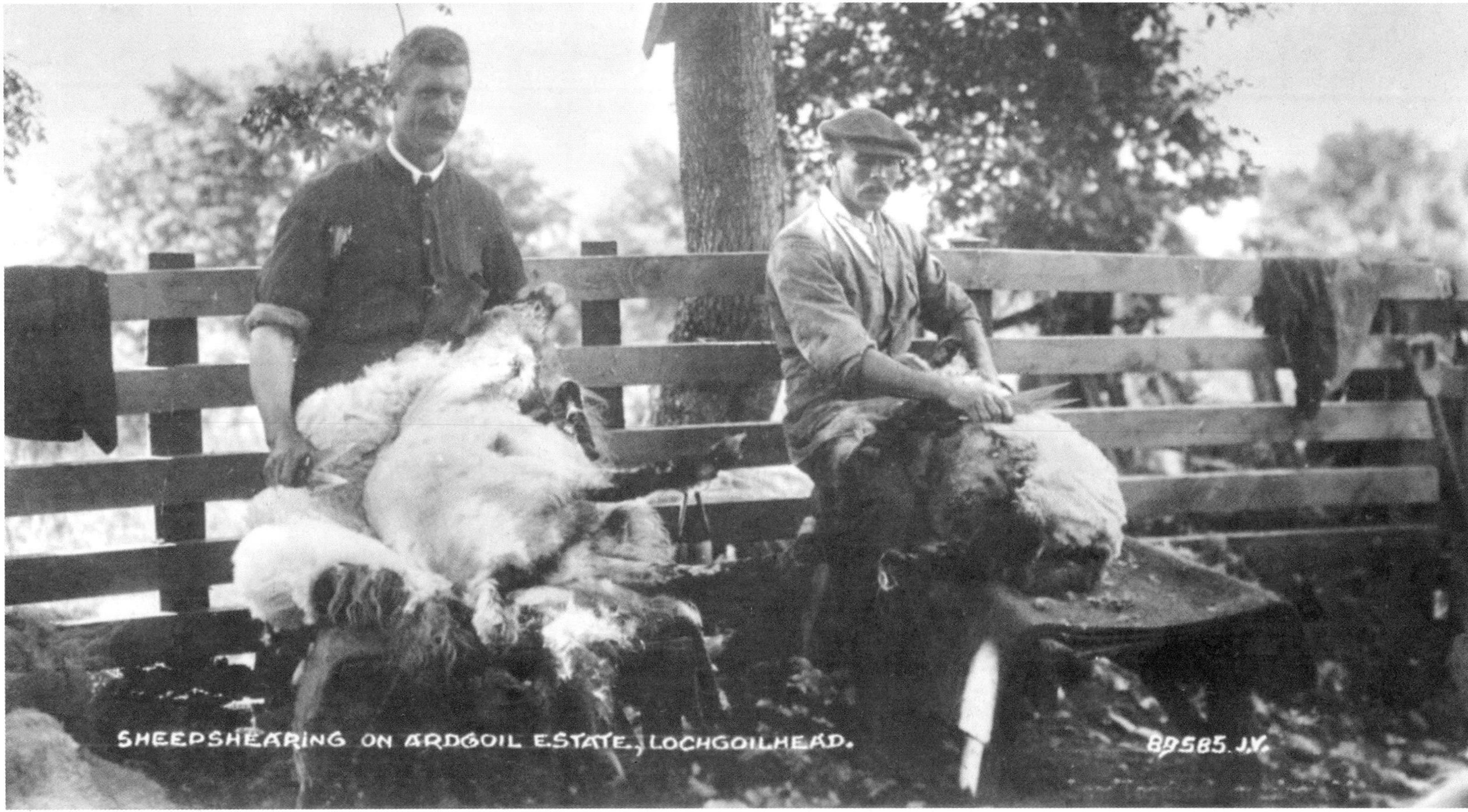


As was the case in many Highland communities, sheep became an integral and important part of the local economy around Loch Goil after their introduction in the early eighteenth century. An early example in the Highlands of enclosures for sheep and sheep runs was established at Monevechadan in about 1750 by John Campbell, a sheep farmer from Ayrshire, who also employed his own fox hunter. Locals viewed him, and other incomers, 'with an evil eye'. Although the immediate area did not suffer the vicious enforced clearances found elsewhere, the arrival of sheep clearly caused hardship and depopulation. The *Statistical Account* says of the parish: 'Since the farms have been chiefly stocked with sheep, one man often rents as much land as 10, 12, or 14 tenants formerly possessed'. Results of depopulation can most clearly be seen between 1750 and 1790, when the average number of marriages a year dropped from fourteen to eight and those of baptisms from 48 to 26. However, at the end of the nineteenth century there were still a large number of shepherds employed in the area – the 1881 census lists 29 and the 1891 census 21. This 1923 postcard view shows sheep-shearing on the Ardgoil Estate, possibly at Coilessan.

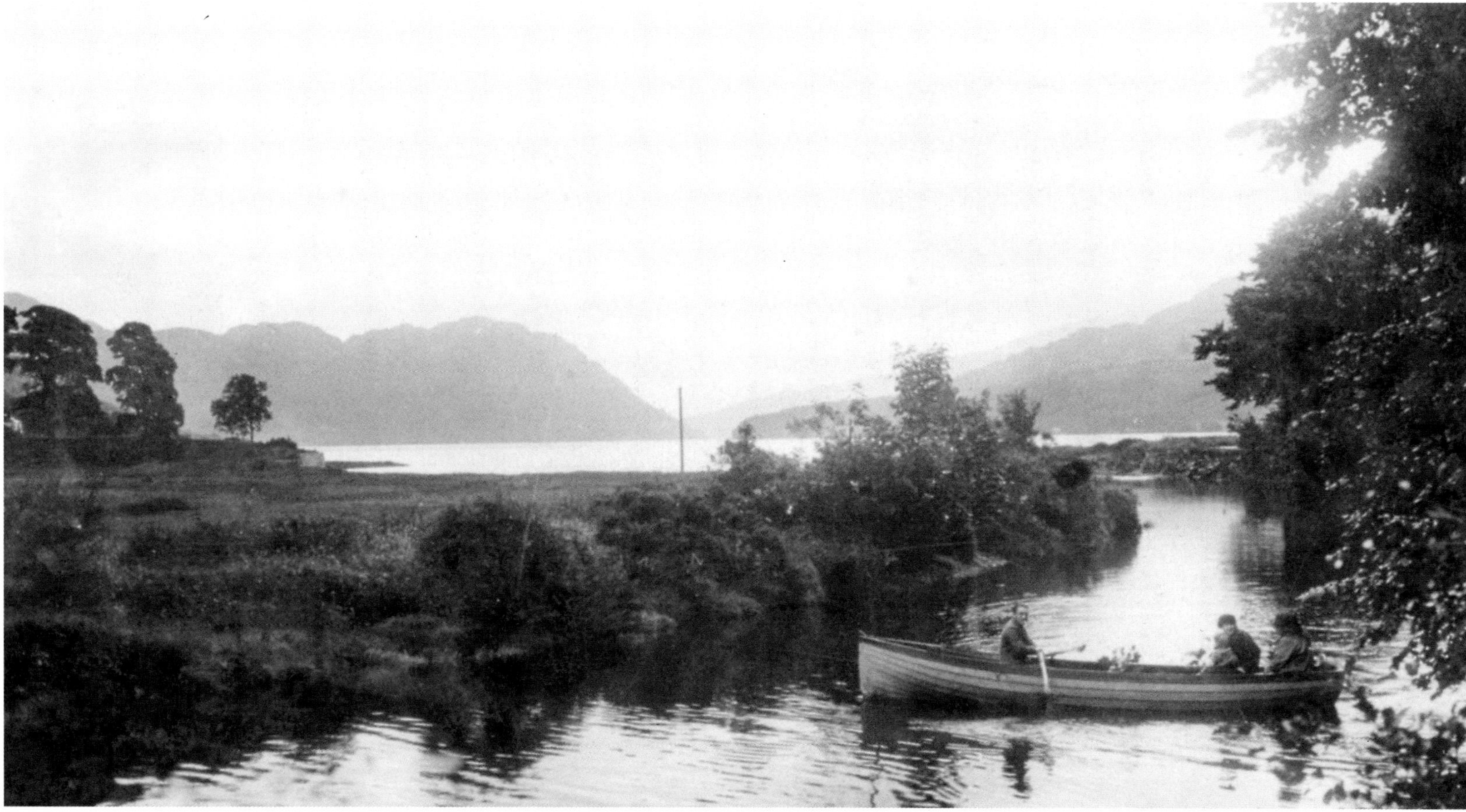

This 1923 scene, where the River Goil meets the loch, is typical of the views of the area that inspired many amateur and professional artists. The best-known landscape artist with a strong local connection was George Houston (1869–1947), whose family rented (for the summer months) the school house in Lochgoilhead and, after 1904, Drimsyniebeg Farm, where his third son, Edward, was born. He painted beautiful and tranquil pictures of the Lowlands and the West Coast of Scotland which were, according to the Royal Scottish Academy's eulogy on his death, 'amongst the finest landscapes produced in Scotland'. A contemporary of the Glasgow Boys, Houston developed his own distinctive style, which was 'direct and simple and was interpreted with a technique baffling in its apparent ease'. Of the twelve paintings he exhibited at the Royal Scottish Society of Painters in Watercolours between 1904 and 1910, five were of the village and the glen. In 1936 Glasgow Corporation bought his painting *The Heart of Argyll* for its permanent collection. Following the early death of Houston's son, John, his daughter-in-law (née Stephenson) and her daughter settled in the village, living at Crag, on Inverlounin Road.

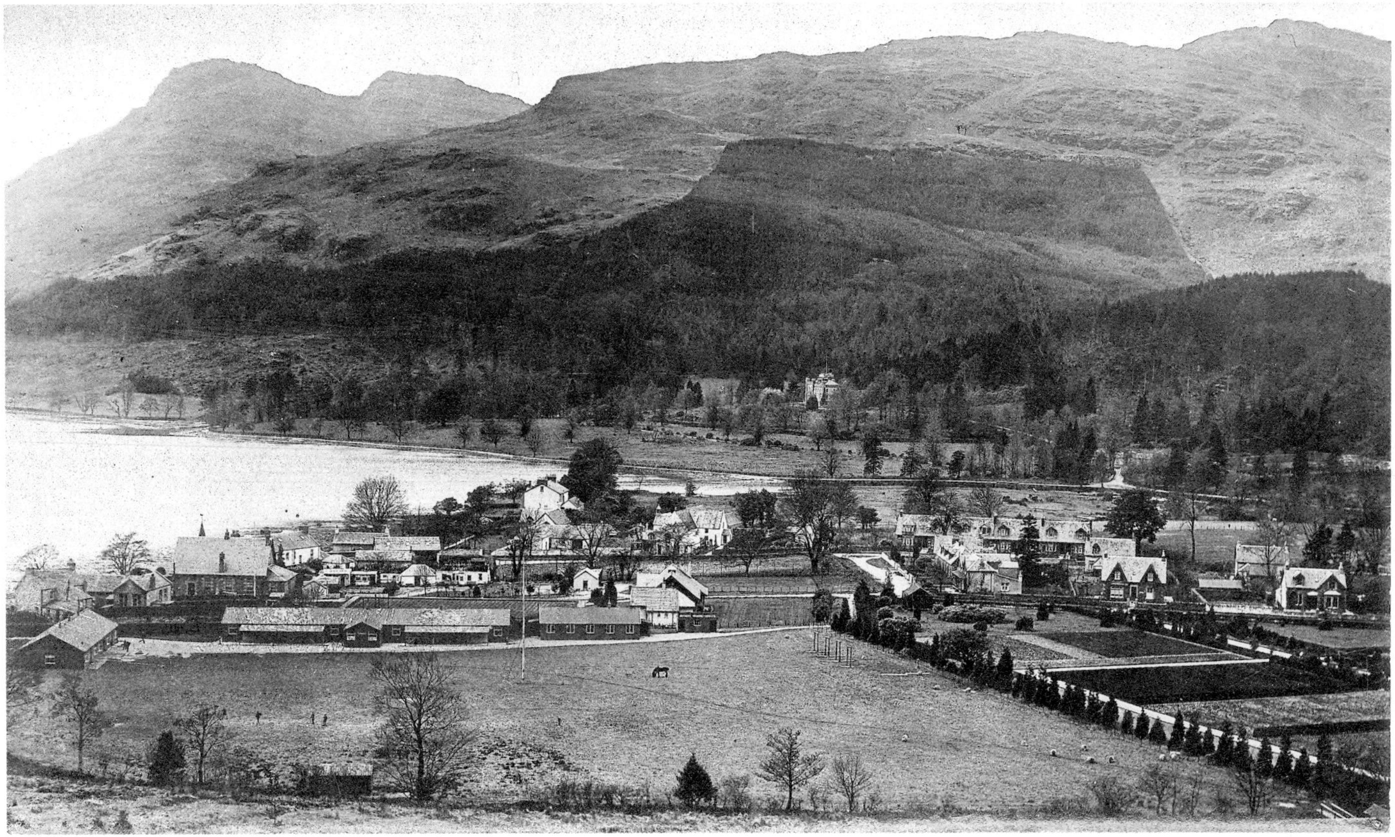

This 1920s photo shows the view across the village, with the recreation ground and the nursery in the foreground, to Drimsynie House, around which can be seen a large variety of trees (the Neilson family extended the plantings in the second half of the nineteenth century). Much of the woodland in the area had disappeared by 1800. *The Statistical Account* notes: 'Old people still remember several extensive woods, where there is not now the vestige of a tree … timber has become so scarce, and so valuable, that … the woods yield a greater profit than anything else which the lands can produce.' However, replanting and preservation were clearly thought important, with 'a great number of trees planted yearly in different places. The natural woods consist of ash, alder, hazel, and birch, but mostly oak … and … Scots and silver fir, larix, plain, beech, elm, and lime'. By 1845 the *New Statistical Account* enthused: 'The barrenness of the ground … is partly concealed, and the tremendous wildness of the scene agreeably diversified by extensive natural woods, which cover the land near the coast, and rise to a considerable distance from the shore.' It also states that 'Mr. Douglas of Glenfinnert has lately planted a good deal along the south side of Lochgoil.' By the latter part of the twentieth century almost all the trees had been felled – a considerable amount of timber had been required during the war – and the mass forestry plantations that are so familiar today were commenced in the 1950s.

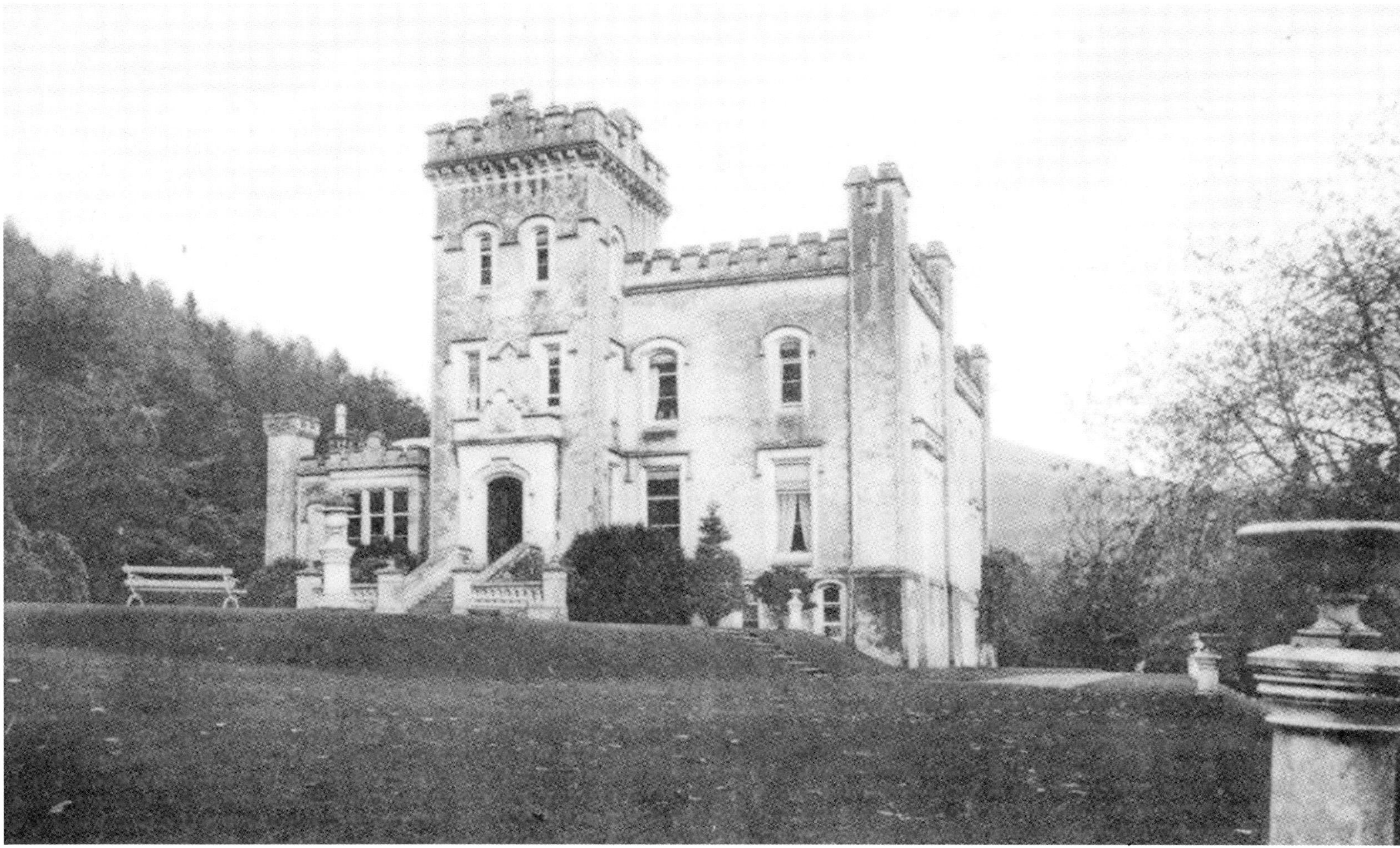

This 1904 photo of Drimsynie shows the house before its conversion to a hotel. It was built in the mid-1850s by the Neilson family, possibly to a design by the Glasgow architect James Smith, to replace the original house, which was much smaller and situated further to the south. James Beaumont Neilson was a gas engineer and the new house had its own carbide gas works, as well as a sawmill with a waterwheel. Drimsynie Estate was managed traditionally until well into the twentieth century, employing gamekeepers (it was a popular venue for fishing and shooting parties) and gardeners to attend to the formal gardens.

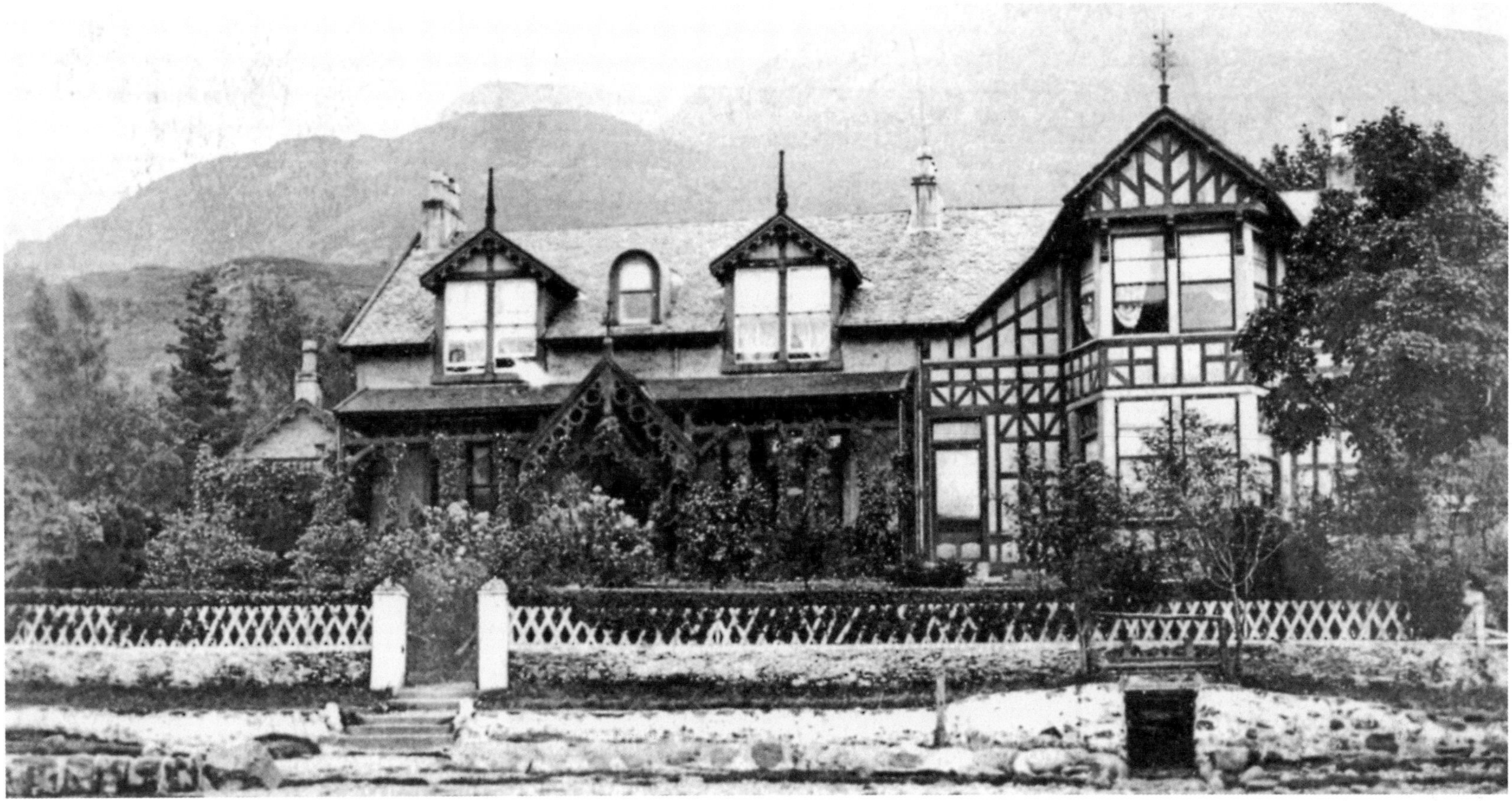

The land on which Blairlomond, near Douglas Pier,.was built was bought by Donald and John McKellar in 1878 from Lieutenant-General Sir John Douglas of Glenfinart Estate, who also owned Lettermay Farm. Donald McKellar was a joiner in Lochgoilhead, living at Howard Cottage, and John, a mason, lived at Oakbank. They were given permission to build three villas, each including a main house and a coachman or gardener's cottage. It was specified that the houses should be built to a value of 'not less than £750'.

Blairlomond, shown here on a 1904 postcard, originally had an unusual cast iron porch and veranda – and the pins by which this was attached to the wall can still be seen. The main house was extended before 1899 with a Tudor-style timber and lathe frontage, but this wing was demolished in 1989 as it had become riddled with rot and unsafe. The 1899 Ordnance Survey map also shows the villa with a pier and a jetty, some remnants of which are still visible. The house was requisitioned during World War II, becoming a billet for Land Army girls.

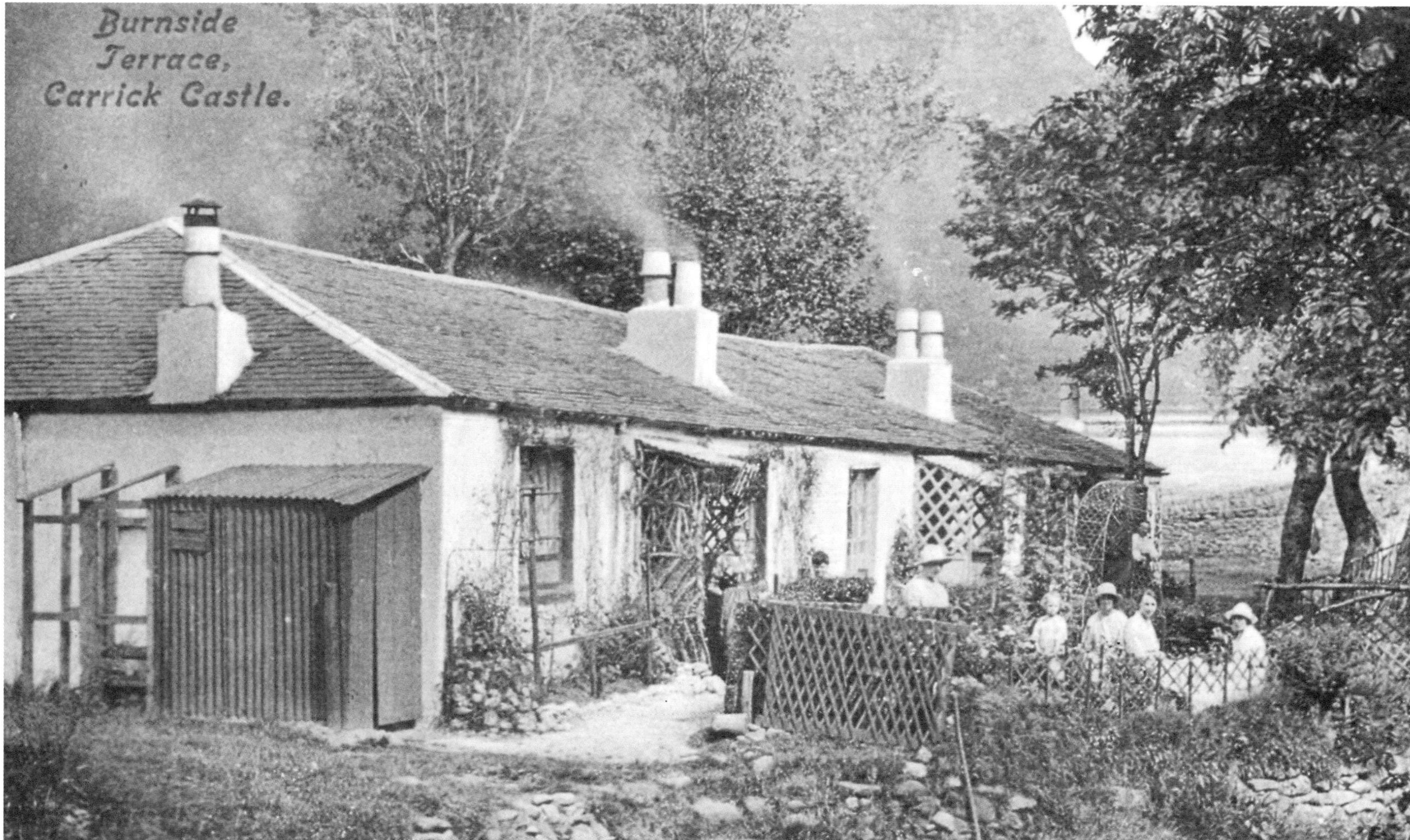


Burnside Terrace is thought to have been built in the late 1870s to accommodate builders and labourers who were working on the new villas at Carrick Castle. In the 1881 census, numbers 1 to 3 are listed as 'uninhabited', and two brothers, both fishermen, were living at number 4 with their widowed mother, even though the house was apparently still being built. The terrace was owned by the Ballantynes, who ran the Post Office at Carrick. Later the small houses were let to summer visitors, as can be seen in this picture dating from 1908. The terrace was demolished in the 1940s and the remaining foundations are under grass at the house called Four Winds.

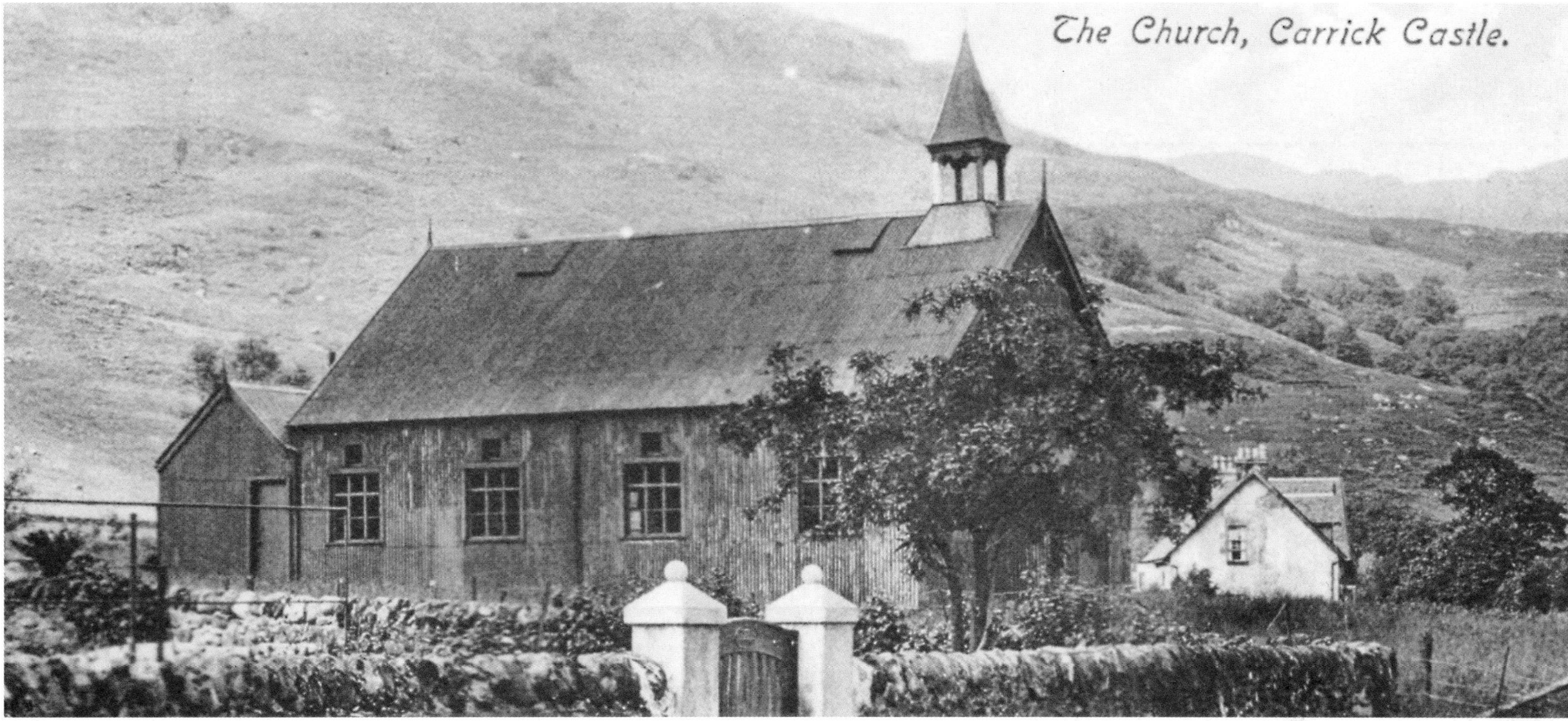


By the 1880s there were a number of holiday homes in Carrick, but those who wished to attend Sunday worship had to travel by boat to Lochgoilhead or undertake the five mile walk. In 1892 the Leschalles family, of the Glenfinart Estate, who owned much of Carrick, gifted land 'for the benefit and accommodation of the inhabitants … as a site for a ... chapel or place of worship and a Manse or residence', but on condition that, should there cease to be a church building, the land would revert back to the owners. The building was designed by John Honeyman (1831–1914), one of the early proponents of prefabrication, and is one of the few of his churches still being used as a place of worship. In 1889 Honeyman had gone into partnership with John Keppie in the firm Honeyman & Keppie (one of the firm's juniors was Charles Rennie Mackintosh). Honeyman's prefabricated churches were regularly shipped to the Empire and the *Building News* of 18 July 1890 reported that he had designed such buildings for new Australian parishes.

Alexander Mories, a Glasgow timber merchant, and other Carrick families provided the materials, and the church was built with the help of local volunteers. A stained-glass window, by Fiona Hammill, was donated by the Craik family in 1993. The bell tower is no longer there and the building to the rear of the church, the session house, is now flat-roofed. There is some debate as to who 'owns' the building itself, but it has been classified as an 'essential' building by the Church of Scotland. Services are presently held once a month, but in summers from the 1930s to the 1960s it was common for poor ministers, particularly from urban areas, to be allowed to combine a family holiday in the area with the responsibility of a weekly service.

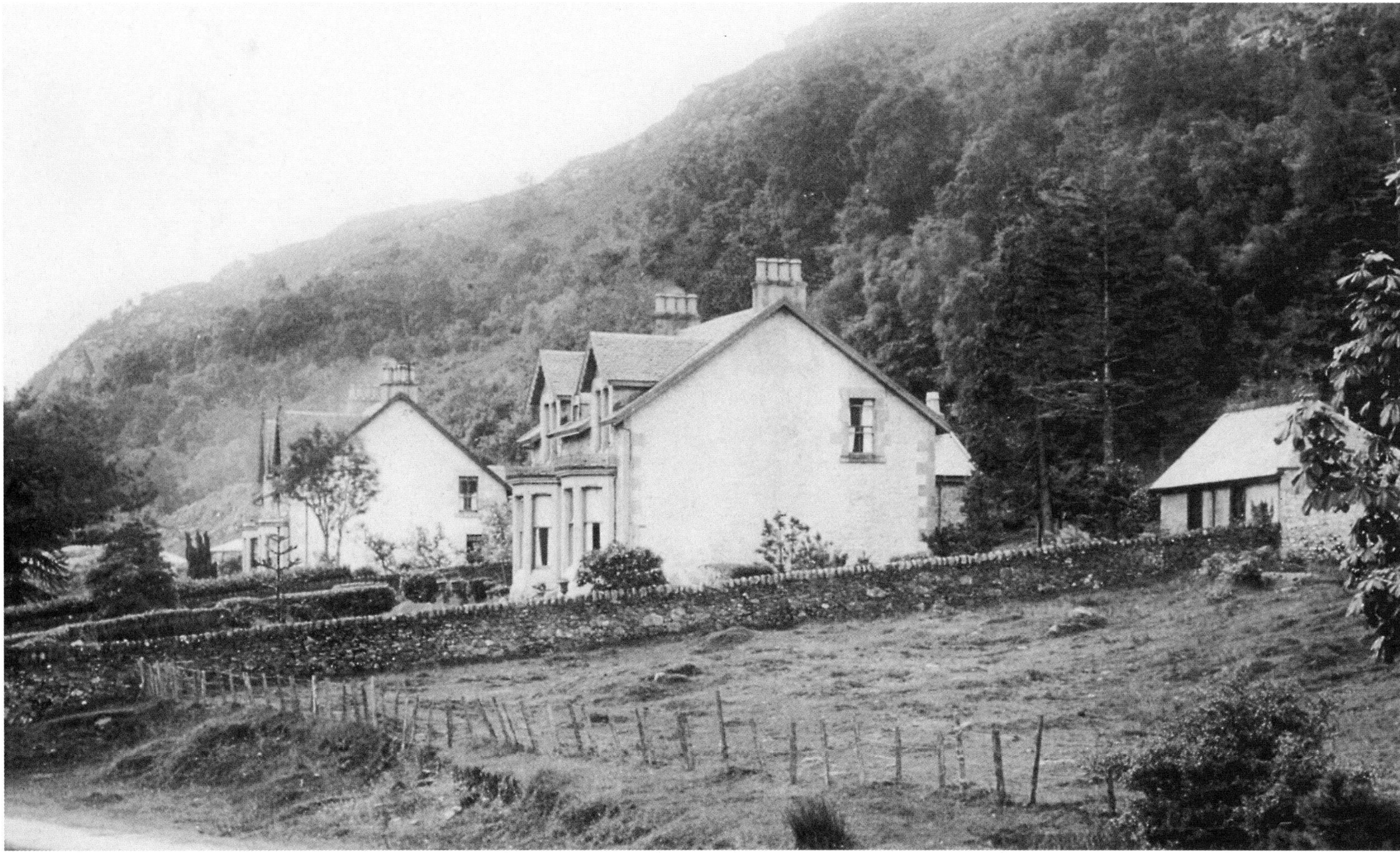

Eastwood and Littlewood are typical of the late nineteenth-century villas in Carrick. In this 1930s view a track can be seen in the foreground. Carrick did not have a proper road until the late 1930s (the road from Lochgoilhead went only as far as Douglas Pier), and then only after the residents had staged a rates strike in 1933. To avoid being branded as revolutionaries, they arranged for their rates money to be collected and banked in Glasgow, to be 'at the Council's disposal whenever they see fit to execute the work'. Despite the Council pleading poverty, the inhabitants pointed out that the county engineer had estimated the cost of providing the missing three miles of roadway at £4000 and that the Ministry of Transport had offered in 1929 to pay half of it. Plus ça change ...

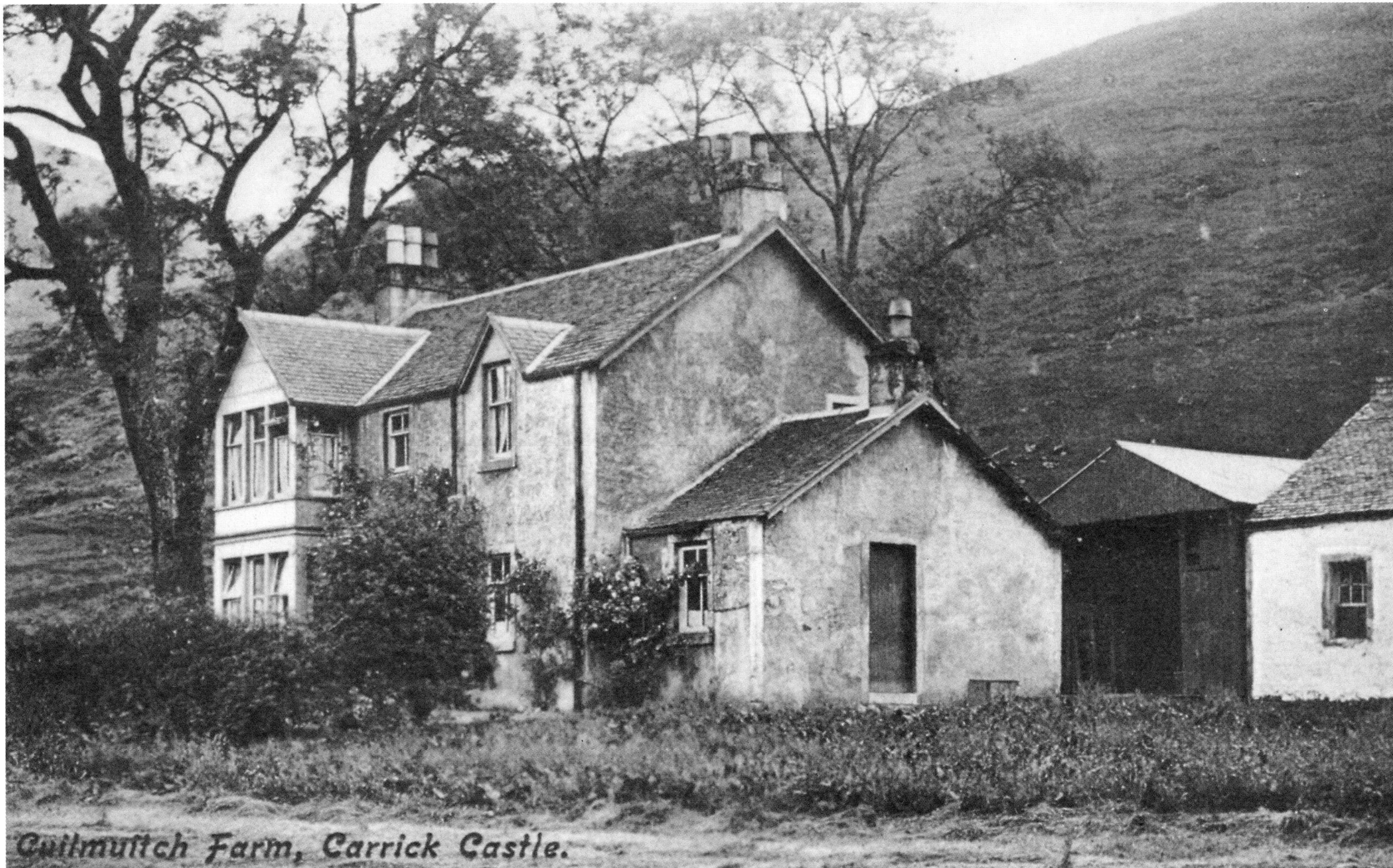


Cuilmuich Farm, along with much of Carrick, was on land owned by the Glenfinart Estate. This early eighteenth-century farmhouse has changed little externally since it was built. During World War II it was requisitioned by the Royal Navy. Ratings stayed in the house and a large Nissen hut was built in front of the farm for officers. Since the 1950s the land at Carrick Farm and Cuilmuich has been farmed by the Ferguson family.

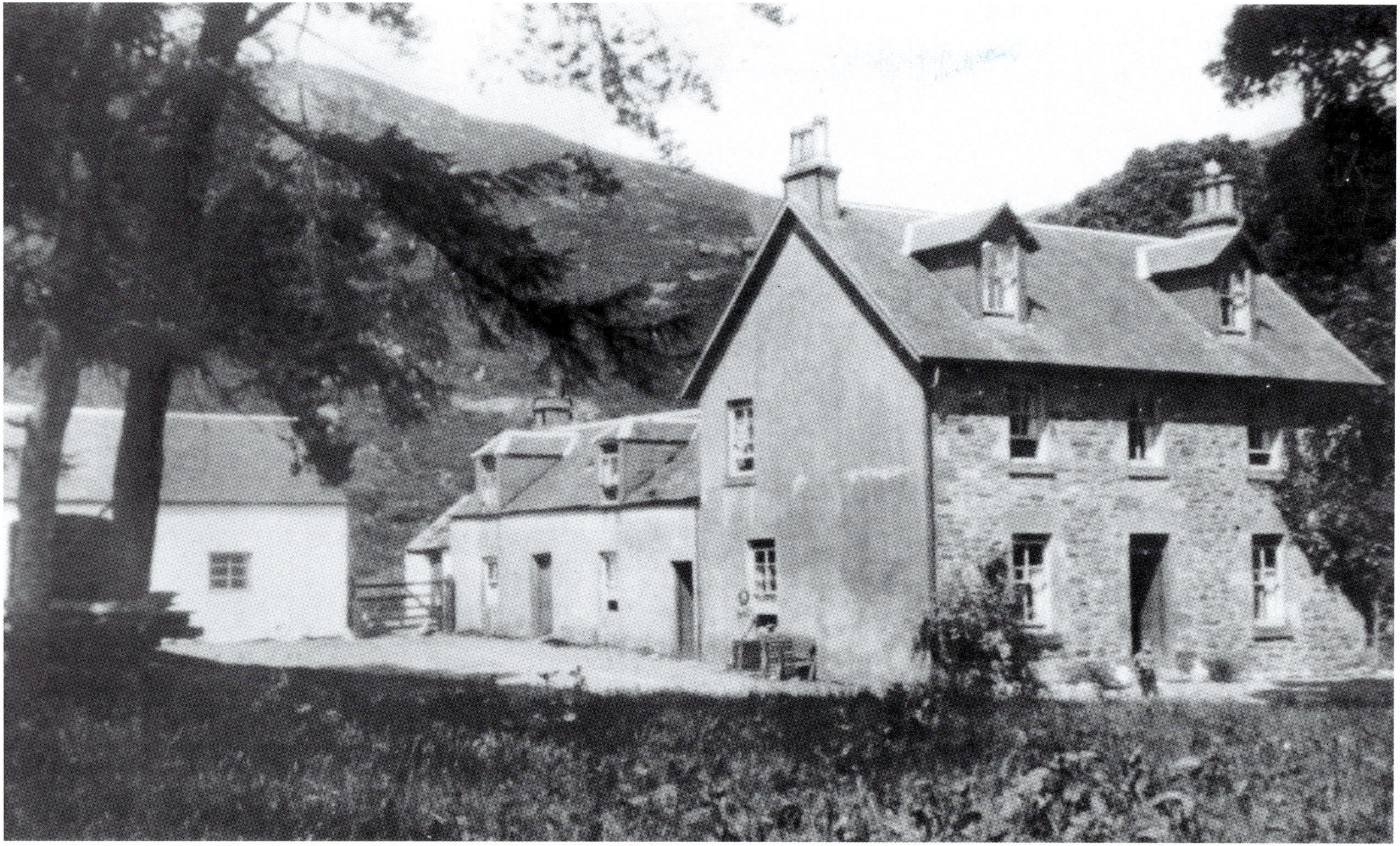

Carrick Farm probably dates from the beginning of the nineteenth century, although it is likely there was an earlier farm on the site. The old steading at the rear was demolished in 1972 and some modern farm sheds were built in the late 1960s, but otherwise it is little changed since this c.1912 photograph was taken.

In the 1881 and 1891 censuses the McGibbon family are shown as working both Carrick and Ardnahein farms. Later the McNicols were at Carrick Farm, before the Fergusons took over.

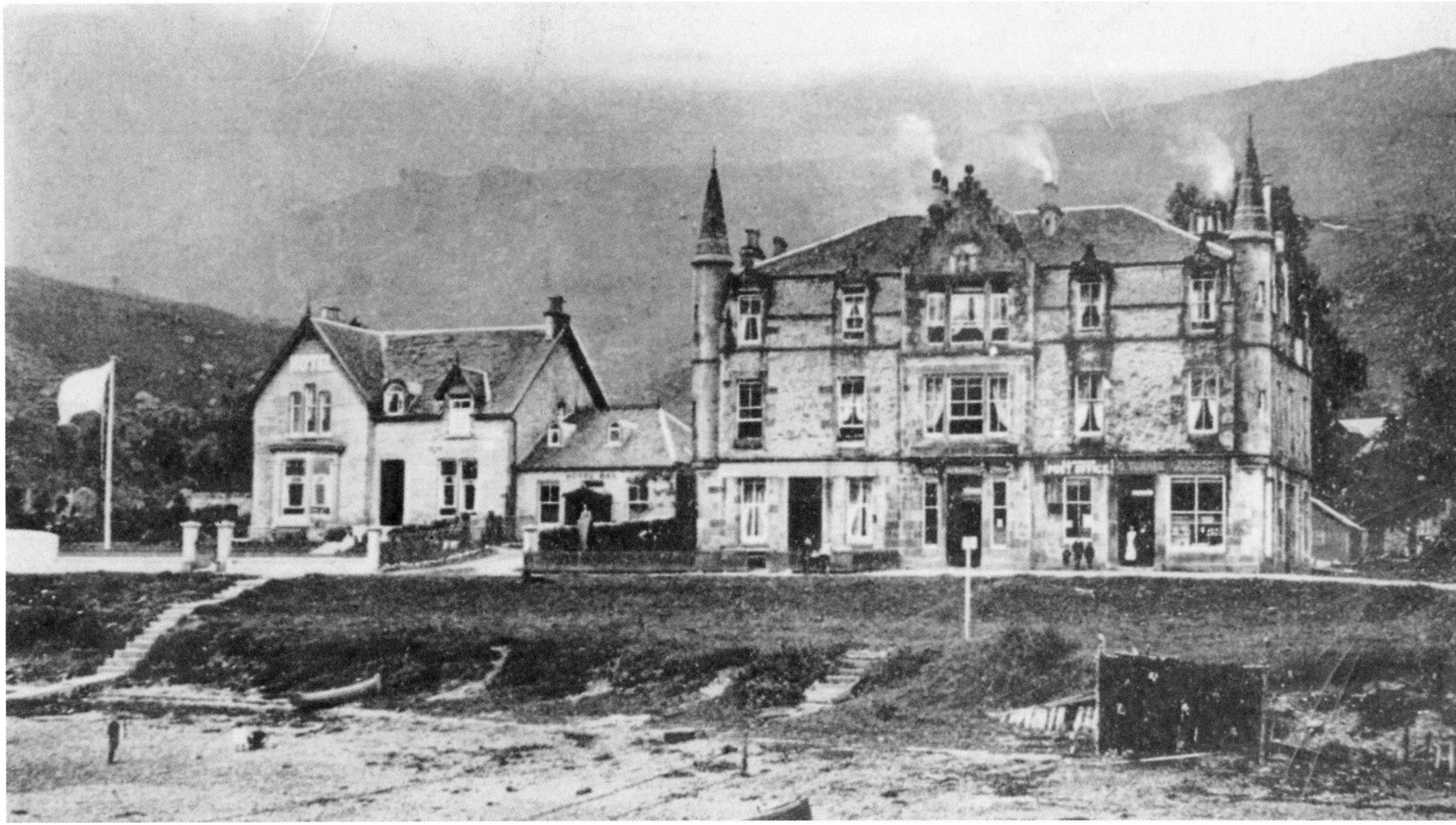

The tenement building (1877–8), now known as Hillside, was originally planned as staff accommodation for the proposed railway from Arrochar to Dunoon, and was built by Peter Ferguson, a mason from Glasgow. However, the plans fell through, although signs for railway waiting rooms are still visible. When finished, it was intended to be substantially larger than the present building, as could be seen by blocked-up doors visible at the rear until renovations took place in the 1990s.

Beyond the flagpole showing on the left there was a tennis court, which was in use into the 1930s. Carrick also had a bowling green and a variety of shops, including a Post Office, a general store and a butcher.

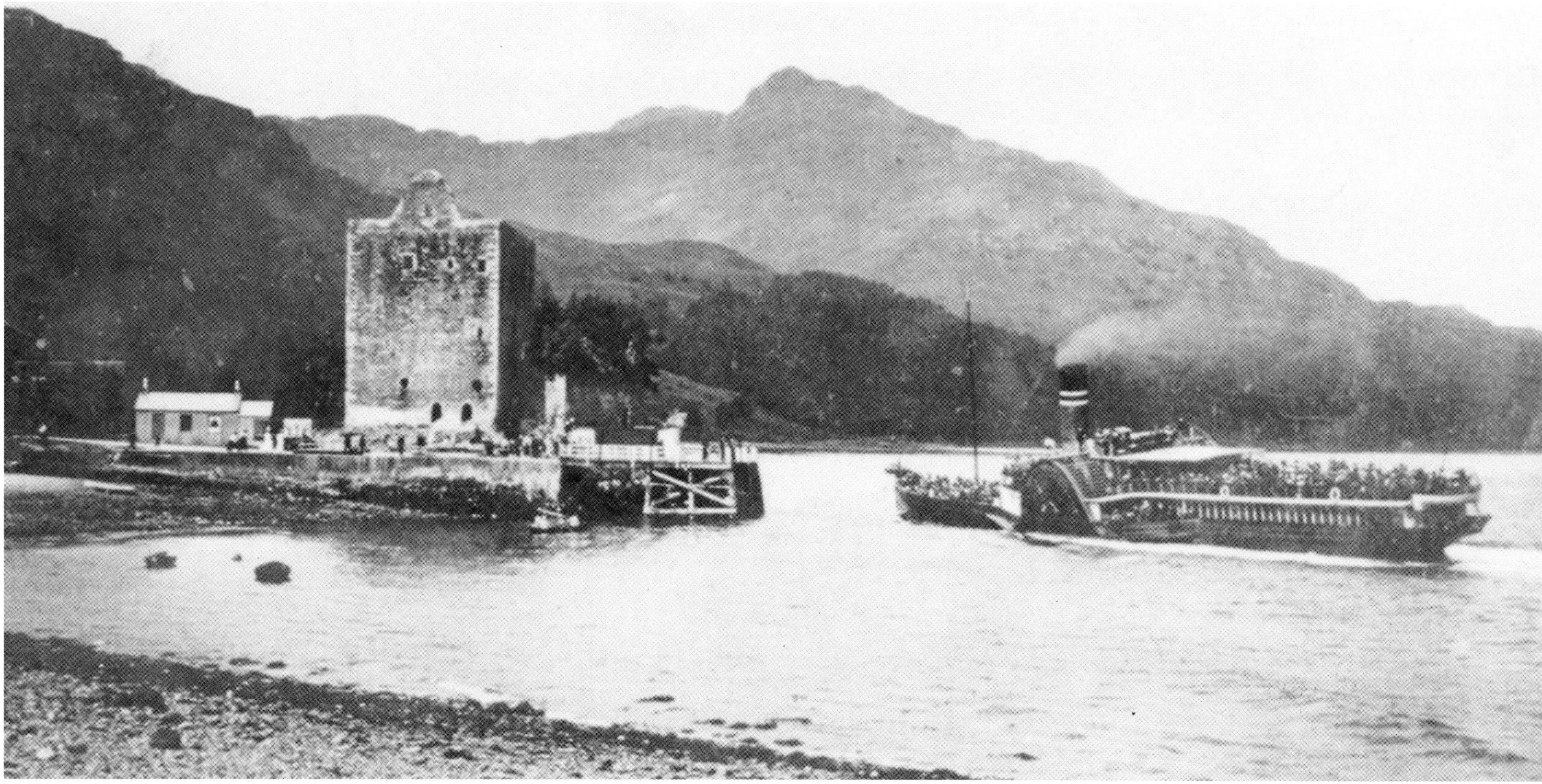

The *Edinburgh Castle* arriving at Carrick Castle, c.1905. The steamer's maiden voyage was from Greenock to Lochgoilhead on 31 May 1879 and she plied the Clyde until her withdrawal in May 1913. She was described as an 'ugly duckling', mainly because of her 22 foot paddles, which were the idea of her eccentric captain, William Barr, a character who appeared with bowler hat and collie dog on the bridge. Neil Munro, of Para Handy fame, wrote movingly about the withdrawal of the *Edinburgh Castle* in 'The Last Run', which epitomises the romance attached to the 'puffers': 'Here was a great historical landmark sent to bed, and not a word about it in the papers! The *Edinburgh Castle* was no ordinary boat; she was a national institution, as firmly rooted in the affections of the Firth of Clyde as are the Gantocks. Since ever I remember she was the most conspicuous feature of Loch Long and Loch Goil; generations of children grew up to man and womanhood in Kilcreggan, Cove, Blairmore, Ardentinny, Carrick, Douglas, and Lochgoilhead, to whom the "Edinburgh" was as beneficent and indispensable as the morning milk. All that was stirring and memorable was associated with her in some way or other. She brought the papers, and the post, and Glasgow loaves; paraffin oil for winter nights; the Findon haddies and the sausages for Sunday's breakfast; orchestras for the balls, guests for wedding parties, the Summer Girl and "nuts" of the Y.M. more-or-less C.A. ...'

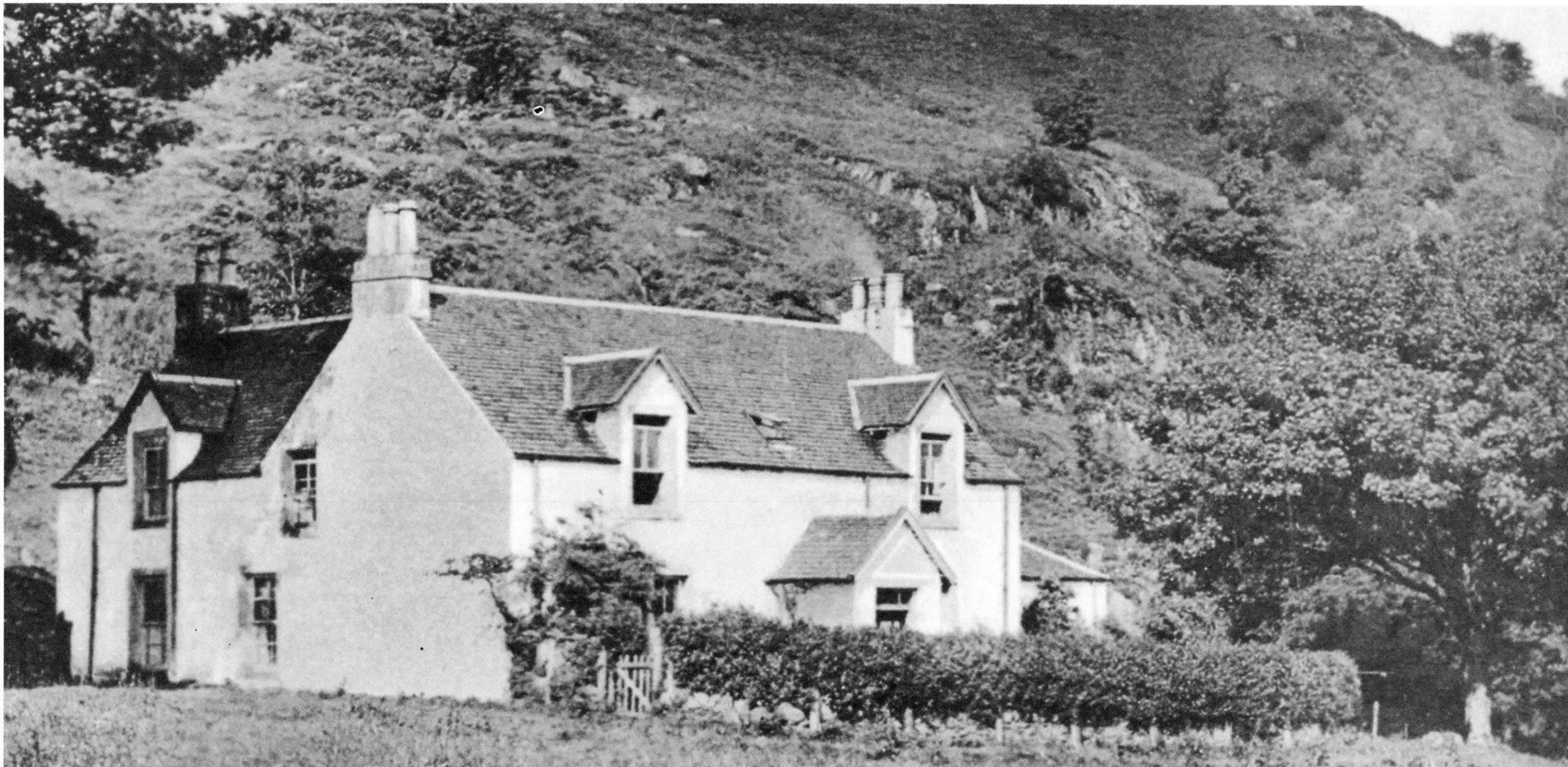

The McPhails have farmed in the Carrick area since the seventeenth century. Although the family still live at Ardnahein, where they moved in the 1920s, they ceased to work the land in the 1970s. Originally they farmed from the Carrick Burn to the headland, including Knap (now a ruin), and mainly ran sheep with a few Highland cattle. Before the arrival of the Forestry Commission they had a particularly sheltered valley where spring flowers grew exceptionally early.

A number of early guide books quote a connection between the poem 'Lord Ullin's Daughter' and Loch Goil, and the McPhail family believe that this might be the case, particularly as Ardnahein translates as 'The Maiden's Point' and is just a short way from the old Carrick–Portincaple ferry. However, it is now generally accepted that a connection with Mull is more likely. Tiree also claims the washed-up body of the poor girl. A more recent literary connection might be that Neil Munro based his Para Handy stoker and engineer, Dan Macphail, on Duncan Smith McPhail of Ardnahein, since the two men worked together in a lawyer's office in Inveraray. Duncan was a top shinty player and athlete at the turn of the twentieth century. Whether true or not, it makes for a good story.

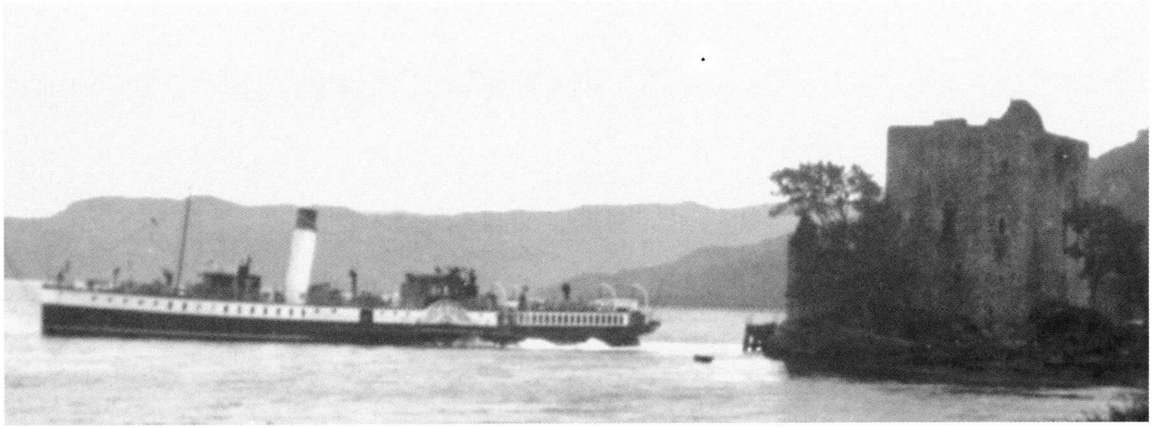

The *Queen Empress* leaving Carrick Pier for Lochgoilhead on 12 August 1935. Carrick Castle was probably built in the late fourteenth century and was reportedly once separated from the mainland by a deep ditch. Allegedly a hunting seat of the Scots kings, Carrick was originally a Lamont stronghold, though it passed to the Campbells in the early sixteenth century. In 1685 the castle was burnt and demolished by Captain Hamilton of the *Kingfisher* in order to prevent its being possessed by the supporters of Archibald Campbell, ninth Earl of Argyll.

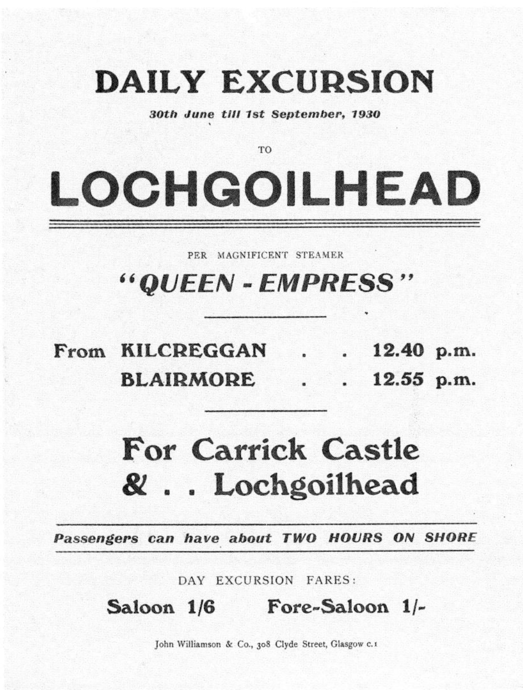


The oblong building, standing four storeys high, is still in a fair state of preservation, having received some restoration work early in the twentieth century. In the 1980s some internal construction was carried out to make some living accommodation. During excavations there was found, within the chamber floor, a massive rock-cut pit prison, which probably dated to the initial occupation and construction of the present castle. The waterlogged deposits within the pit prison yielded substantial organic remains, including traces of a wooden door, complete with iron studs, structural timbers and fragments from several leather shoes. Beneath the sixteenth-century and seventeenth-century sections, some remains of a vaulted chamber were uncovered that predate the military usage of the castle and also fragmentary remains of a subsidiary courtyard to the lochwards.

The *Queen Empress* was launched on 20 April 1912 and joined the fleet of John Williamson to offer 'all-the-way' trips to Rothesay from Glasgow. John Williamson (1892–1919) had entered into private steamboat ownership in competition with his elder brothers James and Alex, who managed the Caledonian Steam Packet and Glasgow and South Western Railway fleets respectively. Williamson was a partner in the Turbine Steamers Syndicate formed in 1901 to manage the revolutionary *King Edward* and remained as manager when the syndicate was incorporated as a limited company in 1902. In 1919 the fleet was merged with the Buchanan fleet.

During the Great War the *Queen Empress* acted as a troop ship to France, as a minesweeper off the Tyne and as a hospital ship in northern Russia, where she was almost 'lost' after running aground. After the war she sailed out of Glasgow, then worked railway connections on the upper firth. The *Queen Empress* spent most of World War II in Portsmouth, but on her return to the Clyde was found not to be worth reconditioning and she was sold to a Belgian breaker's yard in 1946.

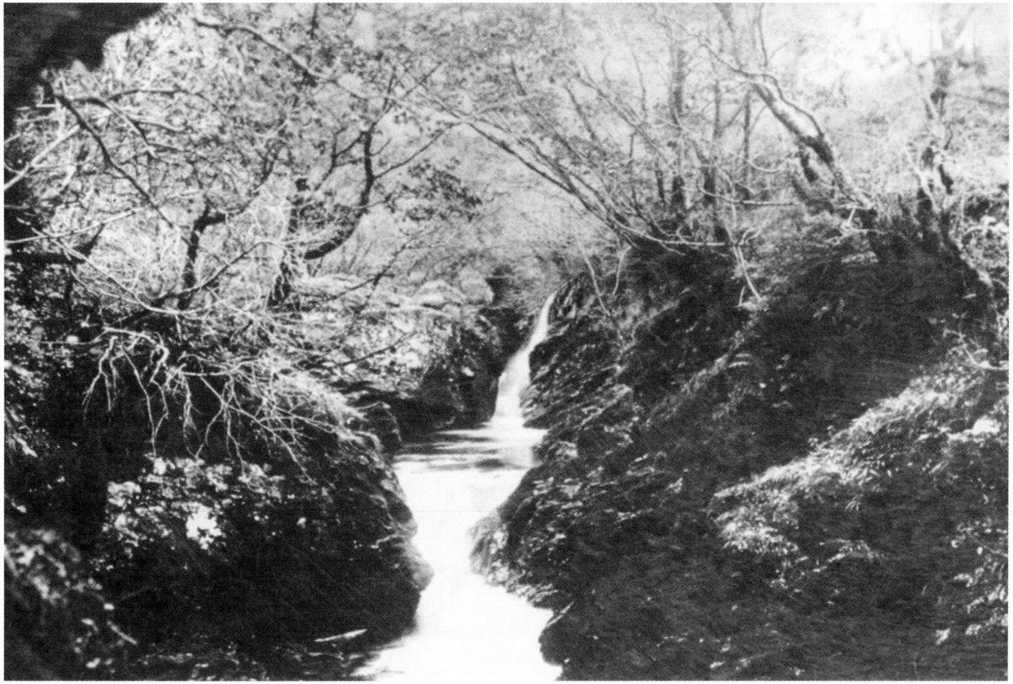

The Witches' Pool is to be found off the Hell's Glen Road down the forest track leading to Drimsyniebeg. There used to be a huge rock in the middle of the pool which was dynamited by poachers, who may have intended to create a deeper pool where salmon would congregate and be easier to take, or may just have been hoping to blast all the fish out of the pool on that night. However, they used too much explosive and the salmon never returned.

John MacPherson with his sheepdogs at Moses' Well, 1925. The MacPhersons lived at Monevechadan, just a few hundred yards down the road. At the time of the 1891 census, when John was two years old, he is listed as living there with his father Dugald (also a shepherd), his mother Margaret and his three elder siblings. The building of Moses' Well, not actually a well but a trough diverted from the burn, was organised and paid for by Hugh Cameron (1862–1903), who was the coachman on the Lochgoilhead to St. Catherine's run from about 1880 to 1900. Thereafter the horses could be watered without being unhitched and would be refreshed for the long, steep climb through the glen. The name comes from the biblical story of Moses striking a rock to obtain water for the Israelites during their flight from Egypt.

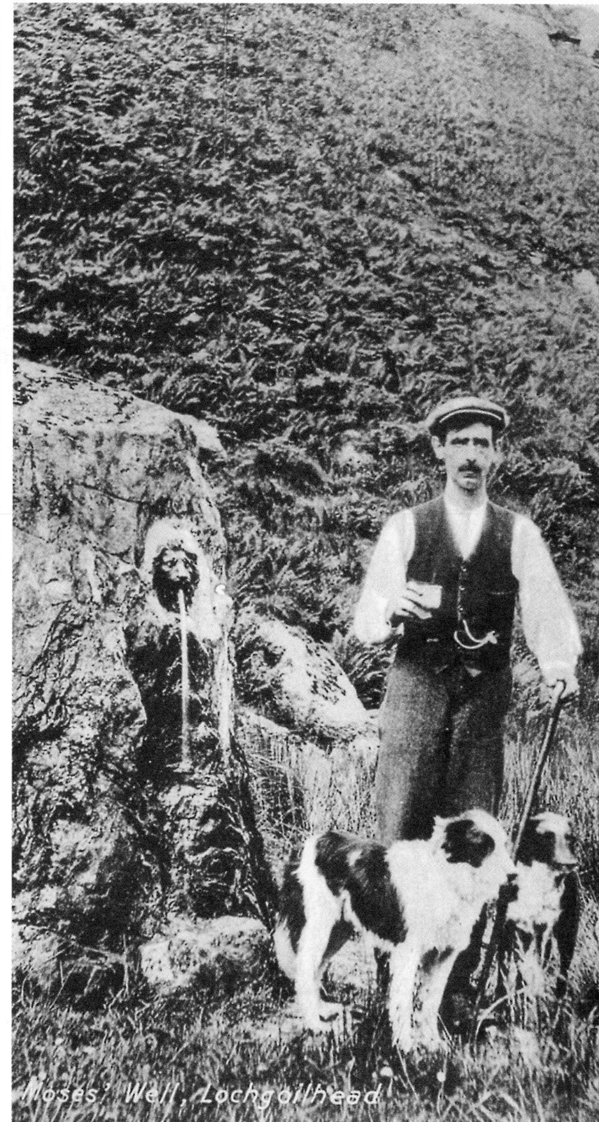

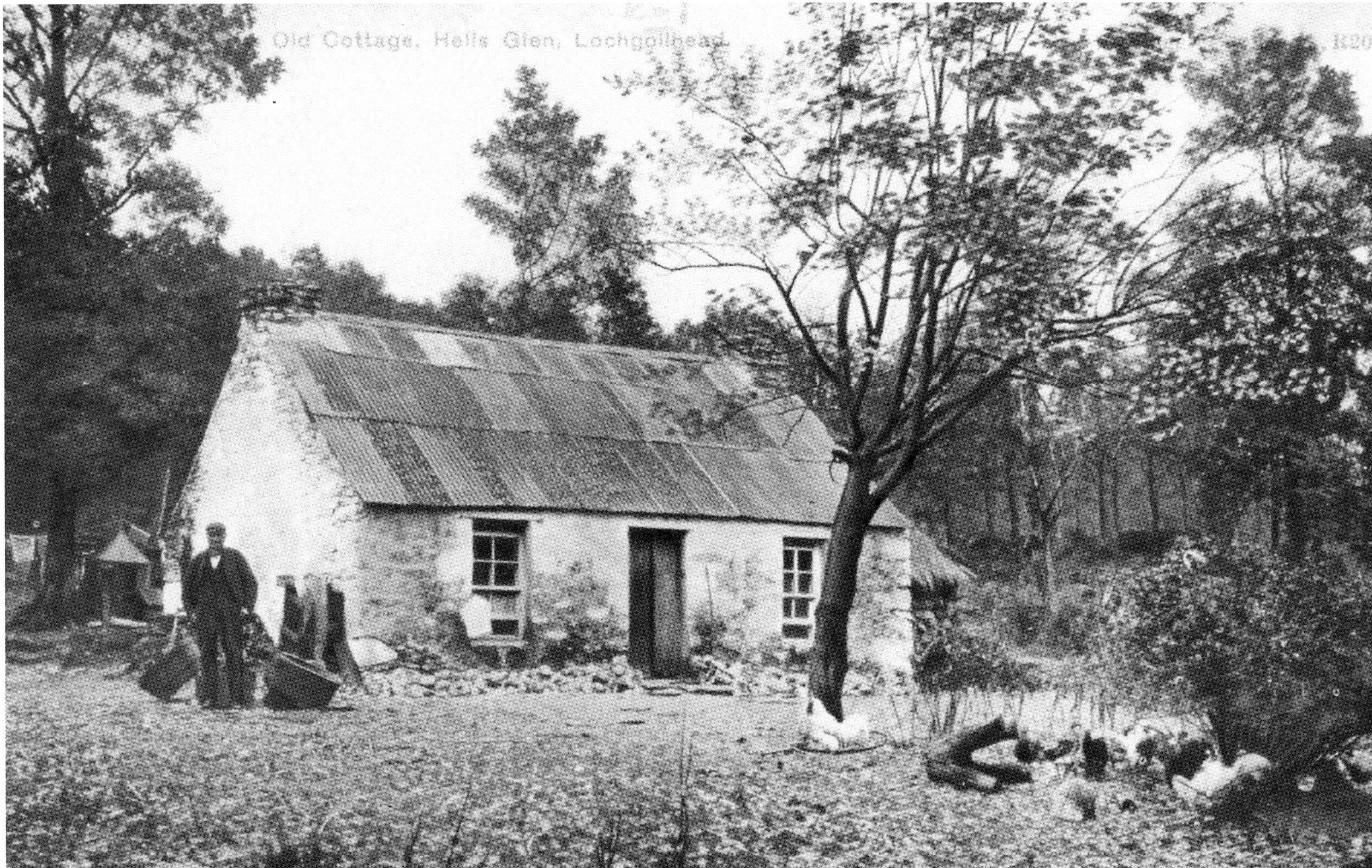


This little cottage in Hell's Glen is possibly the one at Monevechadan known as Glebe Cottage, where the Cameron family lived. The house, of which nothing now remains, was on the old road between the Hell's Glen road and Drimsyniebeg. The last of the family to live there were Betsy Cameron (listed there for the 1881 census) and her daughter Maggie, who both moved to Inveronich in the 1930s.

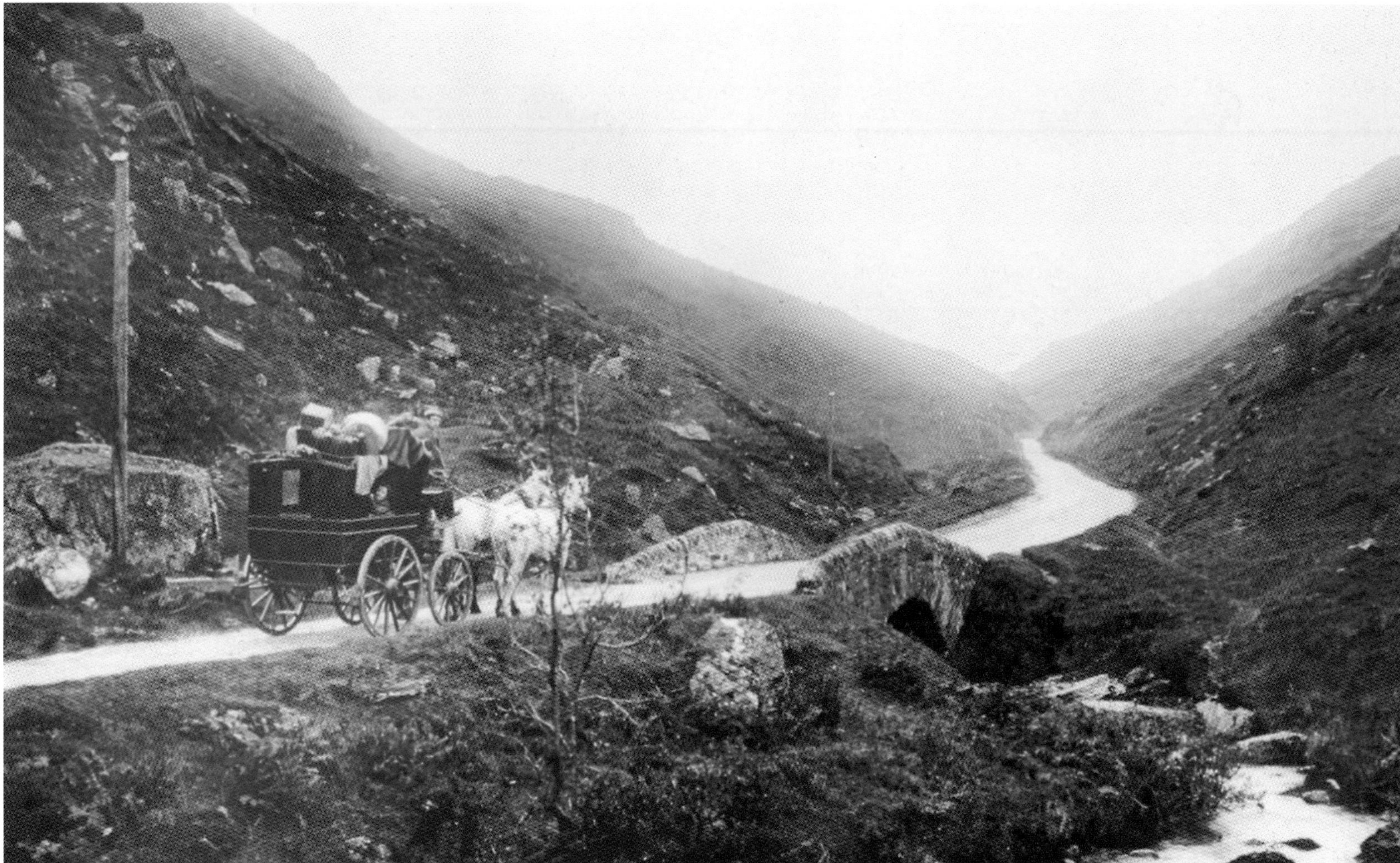

Until 1820 the St. Catherine's to Lochgoilhead road was a grass track, but it was still considered by the Argyll family to be the easiest route from Inveraray for the journey to London. The laird of Ardkinglas and Campbell of Drimsynie subsequently improved the road for carriages and by the 1850s a regular coach service had been established, one of the earliest coachmen being John Campbell or 'Coachie Jock'. In 1865 the Inveraray Ferry and Coach Company took over the route, followed in 1892 by Inveraray Town Council, which ran a small steel-hulled paddle steamer, *Fairy no. 2*, to St. Catherine's.

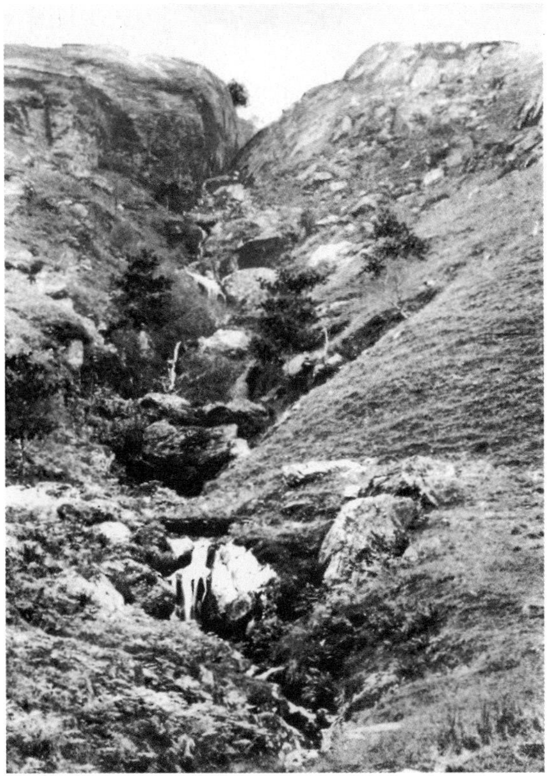

The Edwardian scene on the right is from Pole Flats, near Inveronich, looking towards Beinn Bheula in the distance. The hill to the right of the picture is now heavily wooded with forestry pine. Much of this area was once used for growing corn and hay, but if there was heavy rain the river would often burst its banks just around haymaking time and the newly built haystacks would be washed downstream and end up floating on the loch. As a result the river was straightened and its banks reinforced in 1884, but by the 1950s the river banks had eroded once more.

The Devil's Steps in Hell's Glen are a short way above Moses' Well. Although now heavily overgrown, the bridge across the steps can still be seen.

Gleann Beag has always been known as Hell's Glen. One guide book says that it was named on account of the steep bends, which would have seemed an evil challenge, particularly in bad weather. Another claims the name was coined in the mid-nineteenth century by John Campbell, 'Coachie Jock', who told scary stories about the glen while transporting passengers from Loch Goil to St. Catherine's, but the name predates his time. As early as 1824 Dr John McCulloch, one of the first to realize that much of the local landscape was the result of glaciers gouging out the valleys, referred to 'the deep rude valley called Hell's Glen'. Perhaps the name comes from the 'hellish' impression made by the smoke and fire of charcoal workings, remains of which have been found in the glen. It has also been suggested that it is a mistranslation of the Gaelic name for a small settlement in the glen, where Bronze Age cup and ring markings and a later corn kiln and knocking stone can still be found in a clearing. Yet another suggestion is that criminals being hung on the gibbet situated at the point overlooking Loch Fyne were 'bound for Hell, and that many travellers experience an unexplained chill as they pass the spot'. A more prosaic possibility is that a seventeenth-century map calls it 'Hill's Glen', and this was later misread as Hell's Glen.

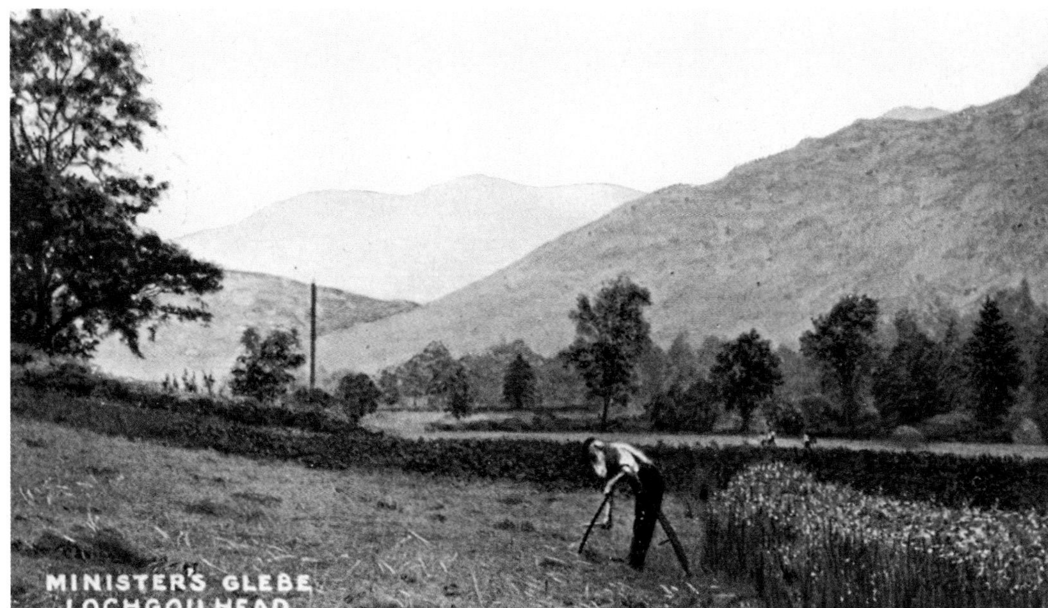

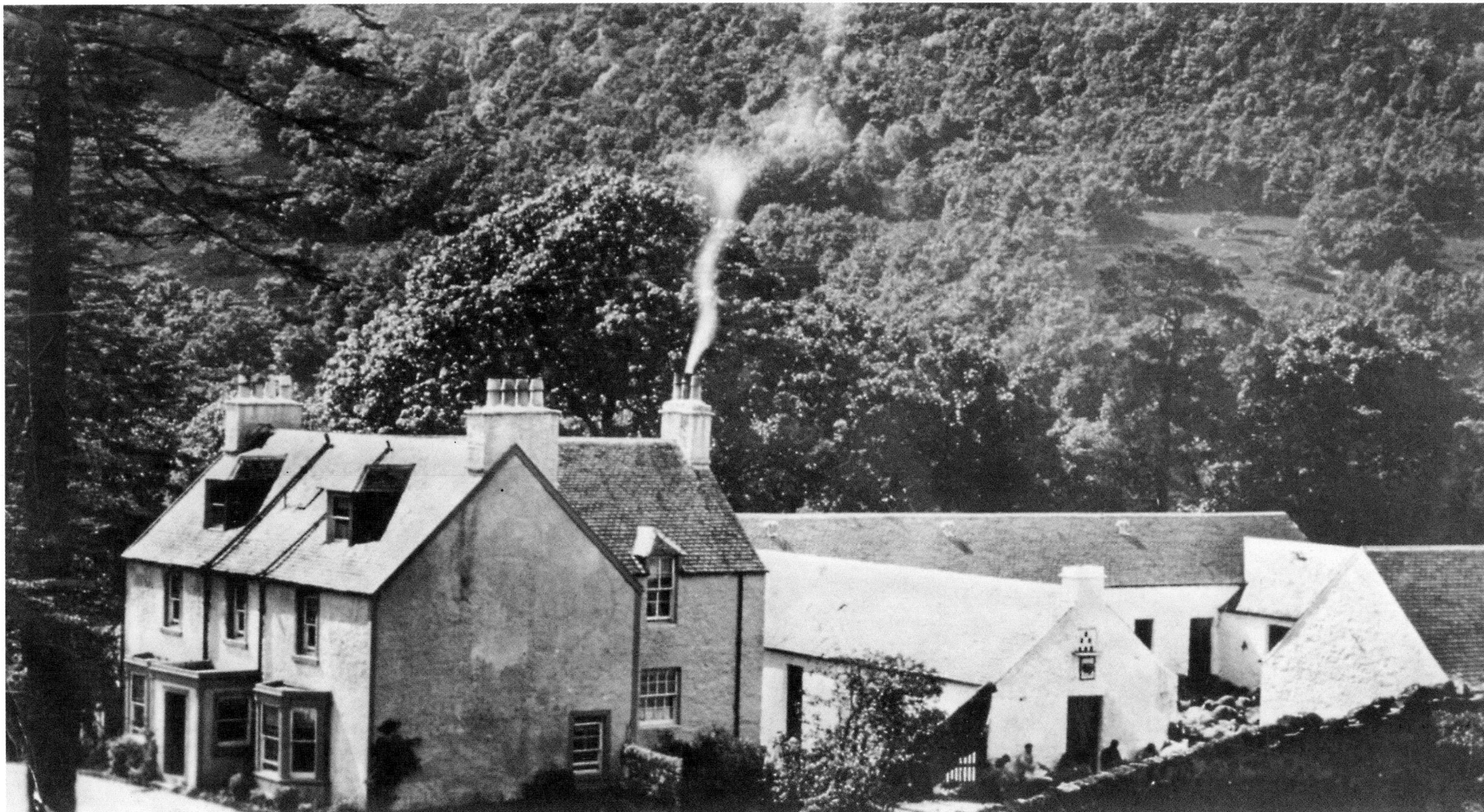

In the 1880s Pole Farm was being farmed by Hugh Crawford (who was originally from Bute), and the land was also worked at some point by the Armstrongs, who were at Lochgoilhead Farm from the 1850s. The present owners are the Jacksons, who maintain 2000 ewes on 7000 acres and also have Highland cattle.

On the gable wall of the outhouse immediately behind the farmhouse can be seen an early eighteenth-century carving of a tup's head together with the Gaelic words '*Tigh na smiorach*' ('smearing shed'). Before sheep dips were introduced, sheep were treated against pests in a smearing shed, whereby a buttery substance called *smiorach* was applied, the theory being that the gooey mixture would melt and run with the heat from the animals' bodies and thus offer protection.

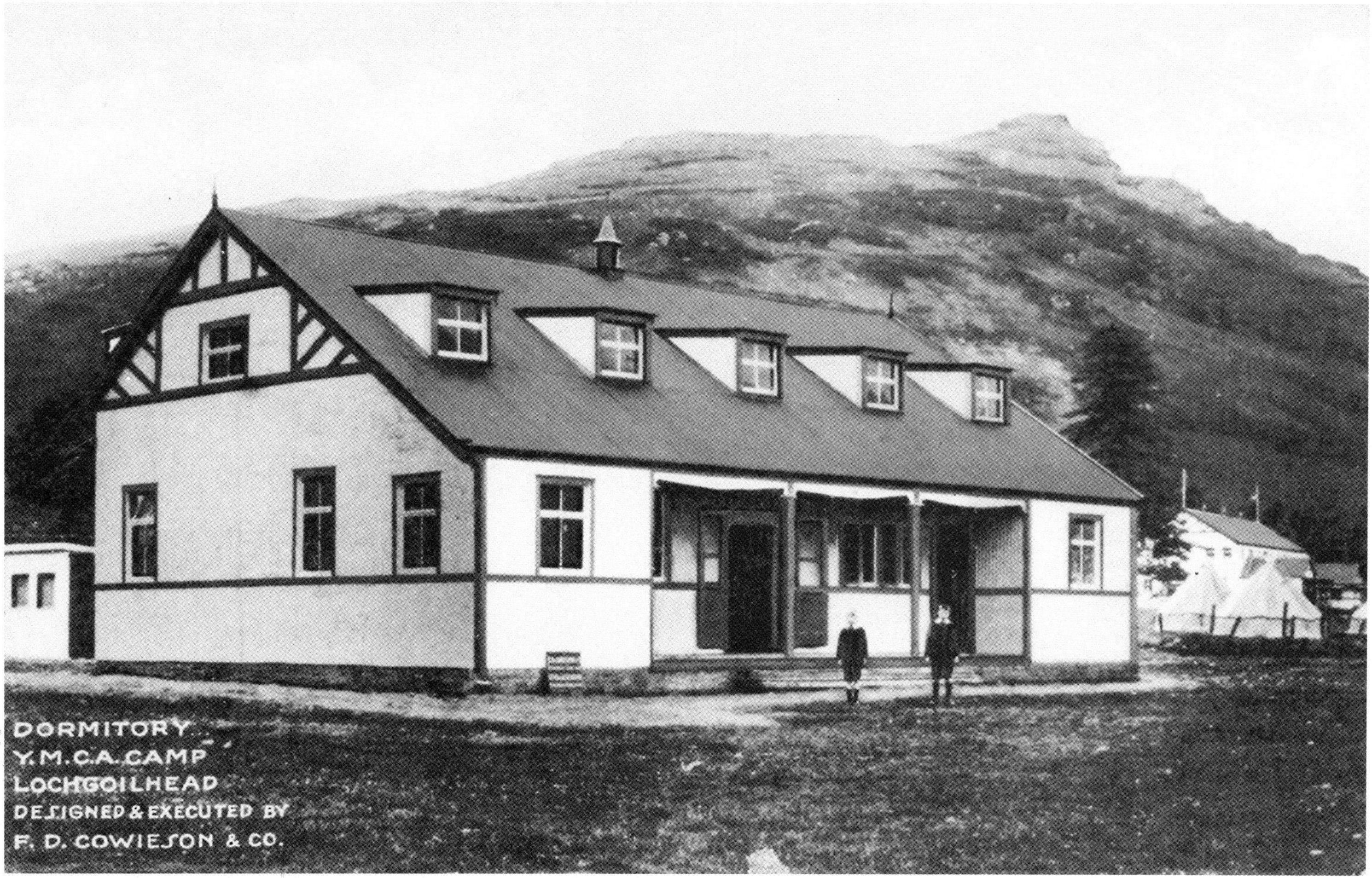


From 1903 the YMCA held a holiday camp at Inveronich every year between May and August. The dormitory building and pavilion were designed and built about 1908 by Cowieson's, a Glasgow firm that specialised in the supply of prefabricated buildings. The dining hall could hold 500 people, and there was a reading and writing room, a dark room for amateur photography, bathrooms, an office, stores, and a ladies' room for the convenience of visitors and picnic parties. Indoor sleeping accommodation consisted of 25 bedrooms and 32 'cubicles'. Outdoors there were bell tents fitted with wooden floors – some had iron bedsteads, but all were provided with mattresses, pillows, sheets and blankets. Prices in 1911 were £1 per week for a tent (with 1/- extra for a bedstead), 22/- for a cubicle and 24/- for a bedroom.

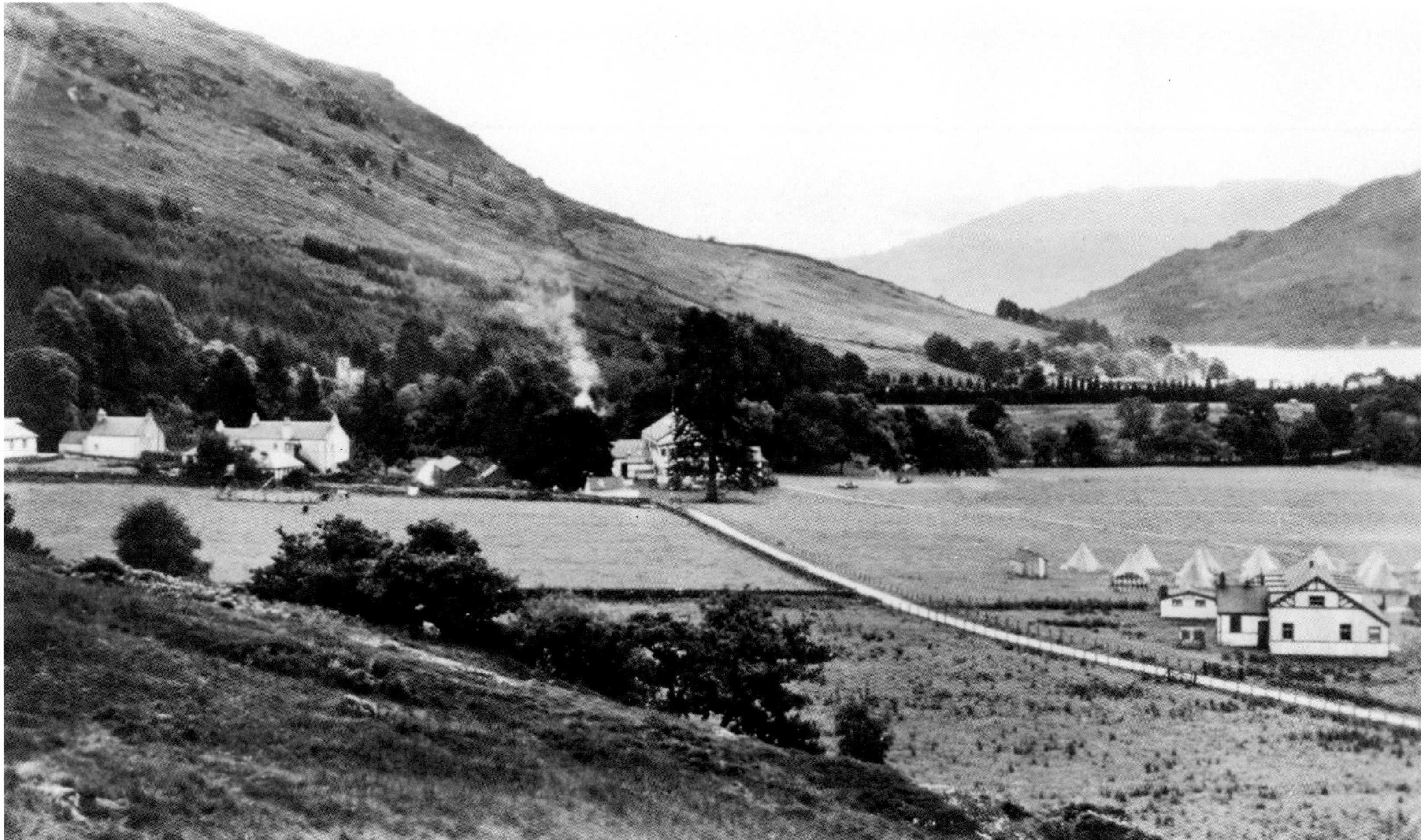

This card from c.1935 shows the extent of the YMCA camp: the dormitory block is at the far right and the pavilion building in the middle of the picture. The camp was host to a huge influx of visitors in May 1937. In the biggest operation of its kind Glasgow Corporation hired four of the turbine steamers on the Clyde as part of the city's celebration of the coronation of King George VI. In a mammoth task, which took nearly two weeks to complete, around 5000 Glasgow school children per day, together with many of their families, were transported to Lochgoilhead to enjoy some fresh air and festivities. On arrival each child was given half a pint of milk and a paper bag containing pies and cakes.

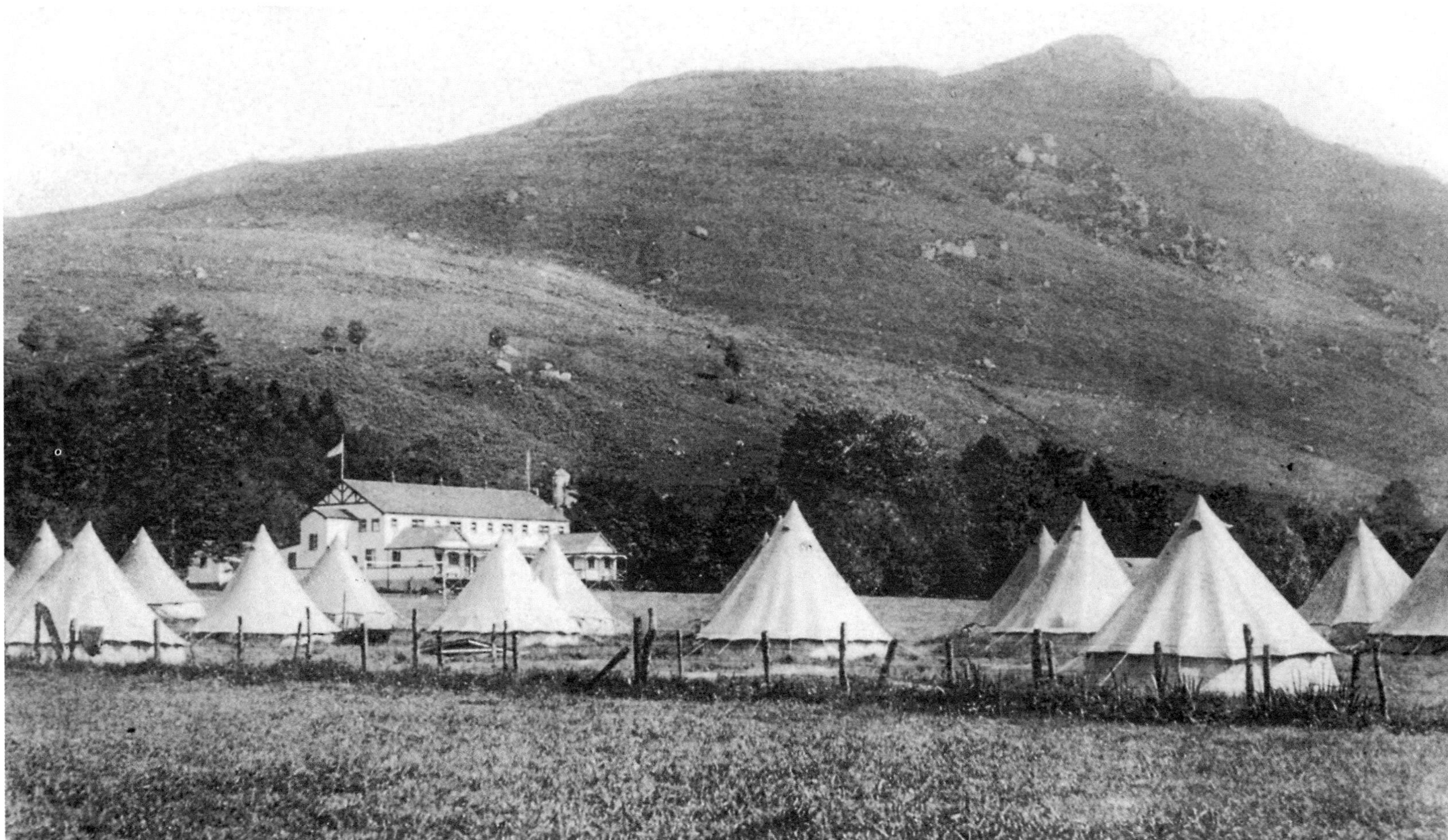

This 1910 card makes camping look idyllic, but, then as now, locals were not always enthusiastic about the influx of summer visitors. One lady who grew up in the village, and was in her teens in the 1930s, told us her parents banned her from going to ceilidhs in Lochgoilhead: 'My parents viewed the campers and visitors as what we would now call lager louts.'

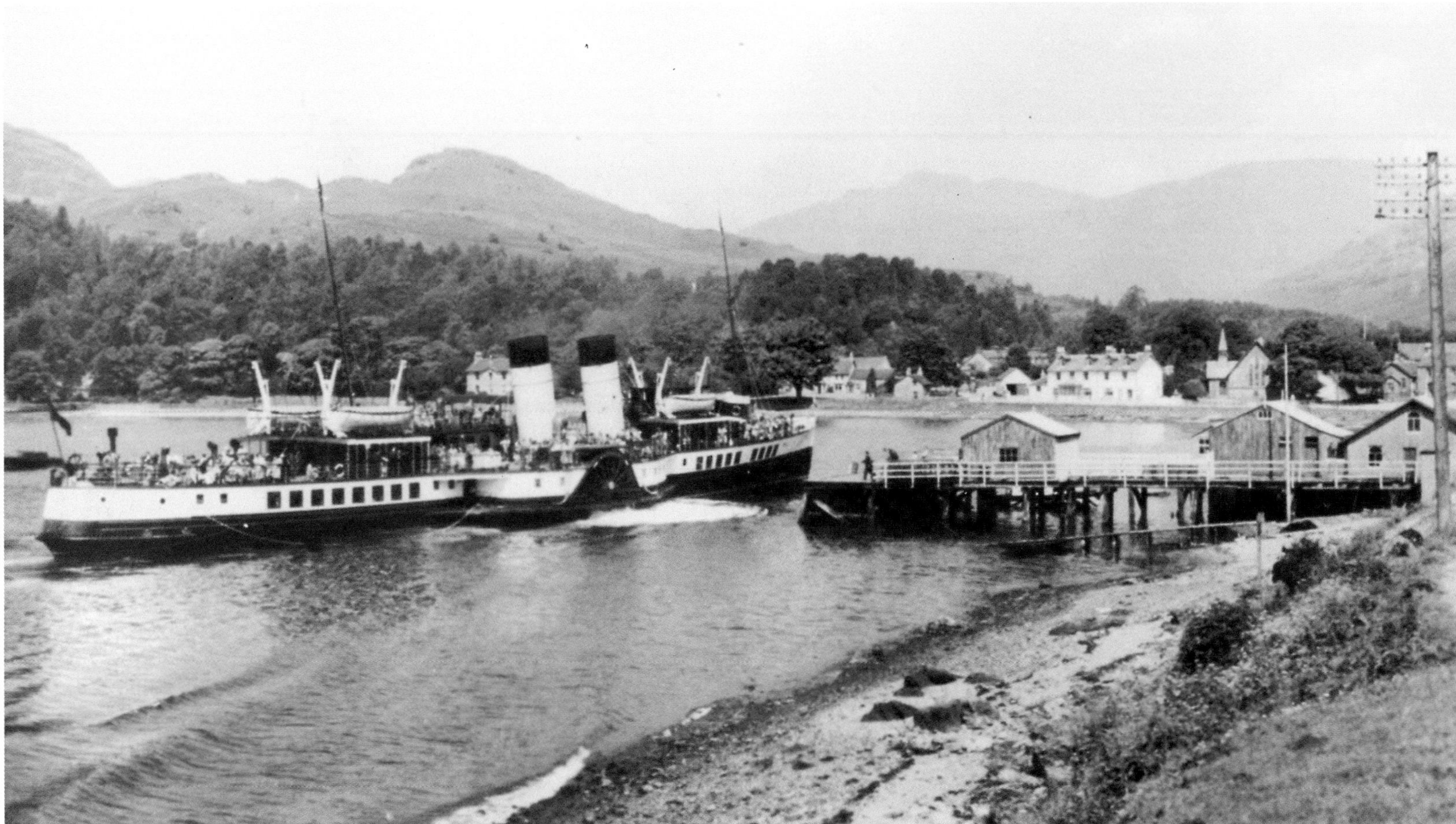

For many people, travelling on the Clyde is synonymous with the *Waverley*. The original steamer, owned by the North British Railway, was built in 1899 and was regularly on the Lochgoilhead and Arrochar run. After the 1923 grouping of the railway companies she continued in service for the London and North Eastern Railway, but was sunk during the Dunkirk evacuation in World War II. Her direct replacement was built in 1946 by A. & J. Inglis, specifically for the Craigendoran–Loch Goil run, and her first trip to Loch Goil was in June 1947. In 1973 Caledonian MacBrayne sold the *Waverley* to the Paddle Steamer Preservation Society for the token sum of £1. She was restored to her original red, white and black funnels and was the appropriate choice of a ship to celebrate the centenary of the old *Edinburgh Castle's* first trip from Glasgow to Lochgoilhead. The last sea-going passenger steamer in the world was also the last paddle steamer to visit the village.

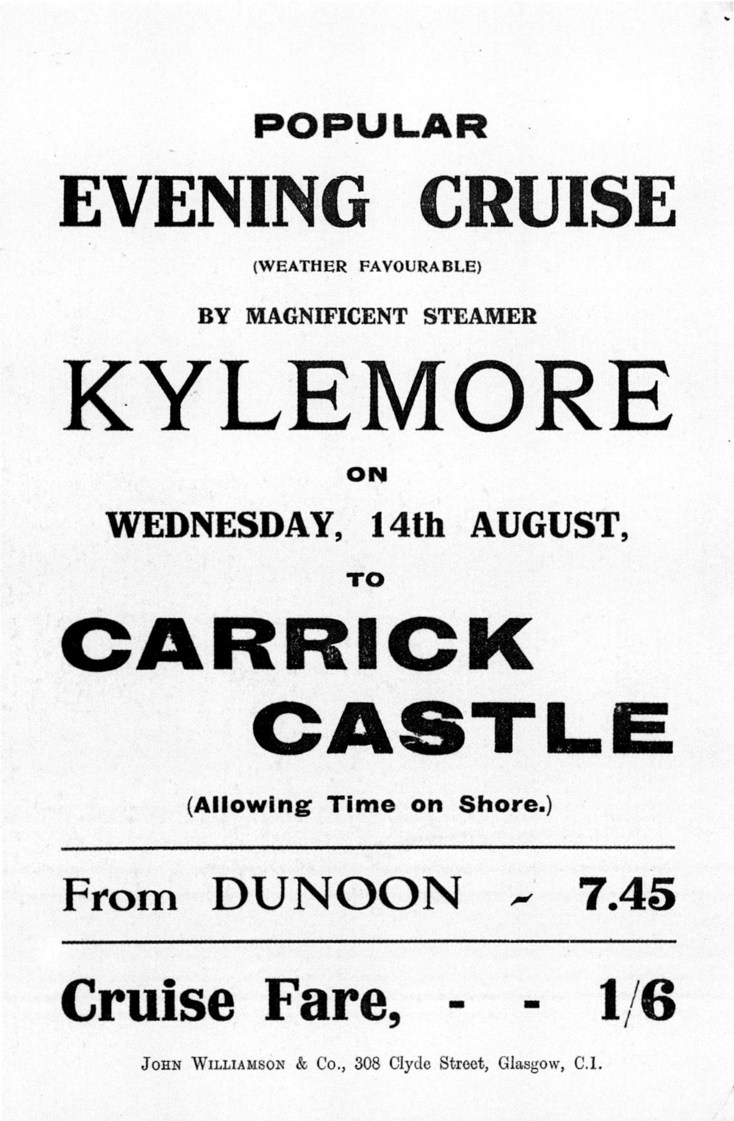
POPULAR

EVENING CRUISE

(WEATHER FAVOURABLE)

BY MAGNIFICENT STEAMER

KYLEMORE

ON

WEDNESDAY, 14th AUGUST,

TO

CARRICK CASTLE

(Allowing Time on Shore.)

From DUNOON - 7.45

Cruise Fare, - - 1/6

John Williamson & Co., 308 Clyde Street, Glasgow, C.1.

The *Kylemore* was built for Captain John Williamson, but was sold before her completion to owners in the south of England. She was launched in 1897 and sailed as the *Britannia* for the Hastings, St Leonard's-on-Sea and Eastbourne Steamboat Company. The captain bought her back in 1904 and she was immediately resold to the Glasgow and South Western Railway and renamed the *Vulcan*. By April 1908 she was back in Williamson's ownership again and had regained her original name.

The steamer operated on the Glasgow to Rothesay service and was chartered by Glasgow Corporation to carry 'eager city dwellers to a few hours of fresh air in the magnificent scenery around Loch Goil'. During the Great War she was stationed at Dunkirk and at Harwich undertaking minesweeping duties, but she was back on the Clyde run by 1920. The *Kylemore* was lost during a bombing raid off Harwich on 21 August 1940.

## Acknowledgements

Thanks to Clyde River Steamer Club, Historic Scotland, the National Archives of Scotland, the Mitchell Library, Here We Are (Cairndow), Ian Broadley of the Royal Northern Yacht Club, Dr Michael Moss, Heather and Andrew Cubie, Craig and Peter Ferguson, Alex Filshie, Davy and Lib Jackson, Jack Lavender, Jean and Duncan McPhail, Anne Murray, Derek Prescott, Jim Sim, and members of the Loch Goil Local History Society, all of whom helped provide the text. Thanks also to Stenlake Publishing for providing the illustrations and for their support and advice during this project.

If any reader is able to add to, or correct, information in the text, the Loch Goil Local History Society would be pleased to hear from them (www.lochgoilhistory.co.uk). The society is also keen to be in touch with those with memories of the area or descendants of people who lived here.

## Further reading

*Statistical Account of Scotland,* 1791–5
*New Statistical Account of Scotland,* 1834–45
*Wade in Scotland,* J. B. Salmond, Moray Press, 1934
*New Way through the Glens,* A. R. B. Haldane, David & Charles, 1973
*Sailing in Loch Goil,* Clyde River Steamer Club, 1997
*Loch Goil: A Slice out of Paradise,* 2nd rev. edn, Lochgoil Community Council, 2004
*Villages of Northern Argyll,* Mary Withall, John Donald, 2004
*The Buildings of Scotland: Argyll and Bute,* Frank Arneil Walker, Yale University Press, 2005